# Rhubarb, Royalty and the Story of the

The B1222 is part of the network of almost 20 000 miles of such roads that criss-cross the UK. It modestly winds its way over about twenty miles of the Vale of York. But in so doing it passes a fine carving of the face of Henry II at Stillingfleet, the 'Windsor of the North' at Cawood, and Anglo-Saxon King Athelstan's palace at Sherburn. Three royal references in less than thirty miles...that'll do for me!

Not content to rest on royal laurels, the B1222 also breezes by a centre of rhubarb research, a space probe to Saturn and through a proud Celtic kingdom.

What's more, I've lived most of my adult life close to the B1222 and have enjoyed discovering its histories and mysteries. Thus, I set about researching and recording the B1222's doings, to expose others to the wonders of its curves, contours and carriageways.

The result, dear reader, is this slim tome, which I hope will inspire you to venture out on your own gentle exploration along this beguiling back road.

*David Lewis*

David Lewis : Cawood : Spring 2021.

Yorkshire Philosophical Society   April '23

Published in the United Kingdom by
David Lewis, 32 Church End, Cawood, Selby YO8 3SN
Content and illustrations © David Lewis 2021 (unless shown otherwise)
All Rights Reserved
No portion of this book may be reproduced, stored in a retrieval system or transmitted by any means
without the prior written permission of the publisher.
The right of David Lewis to be identified as the author of this work has been asserted by him in
accordance with the Copyright, Design and Patents Act 1988
First published : 7.7.21
Second edition, with additions and corrections, June 2022
ISBN 978-1-5272-9580-3
Contact email : rrros1222@gmail.com

Outside cover : Backdrop : Cawood Bridge. Insert images : Saturn marker on Solar System cycleway at Naburn, Road sign at Fulford.

Inside rear cover : A pre-1960s sign, formerly at the Kirkgate/Low Street junction in Sherburn.

Contents page : Backdrop  : "Fisher of Dreams" sculpture at Naburn

*A selection of finest Cawood - grown rhubarb*

# Contents

# Why is the B1222 special?

In many ways, the B1222 is an entirely 'normal' B road, travelling, as it does, through pleasant countryside and welcoming villages for around twenty miles or so, in performing its designated role of linking two A roads. It is of reasonable length and has kept its integrity since designation in the 1920s. All in all, just a small component of the 20 000 or so miles of B roads in the UK and an ideal candidate for the study of such highways should you feel so inclined.

But, as I hope the text that follows will reveal, in its winding course, it graces the scene of more historic events than a normal distributor road could be expected to , and so, it might be argued, the B1222 is exceptional.

The reality is, however, much more romantic. I have lived in Cawood, bisected by the B1222, for over half of my adult life, and came to see it as a welcoming companion on my way to and from university, to and from visiting friends and family, to and from hospital for the birth of my daughter and to and from work.

So, this book is a form of homage to the many times, reasons and occasions I have traversed its tarmac. This book is also dedicated to all those who have passed along its way. For those familiar with its joys, perhaps you will uncover some facts of which you were unaware. For those new to the road, welcome to twenty miles of discoveries!

# Introduction, Notes, Acknowledgements, Tour and Transit details

Before starting to explore, it seems appropriate to explain how I have set out this book.

Firstly, this general introduction describes the background.

A section explaining the road-numbering system that gave the B1222 its identity then follows. If such a technical discussion is not of interest, move directly to the "Tours" and "Transits" section, where the road itself and that which it passes are discussed.

This is the core of the book. A series of 'Tours' linked by a series of 'Transits' in a journey west from Fulford. The 'tours' are suggestions of where you might stop off and what you might see and the 'transits' concern themselves with what is going on between 'tour' venues.

Finally, there is a brief list of the most vital websites and books consulted - although of course, these days, just googling any particular item will bring up more possible links than any reference section could reasonably list.

Given that the B1222 is about twenty miles from end to end, a keen walker could go from end to end in a day. However, this is avowedly **not** the aim of this book. As there are many places where there is no pavement, there are blind bends aplenty and in parts the road is barely wide enough to meet the ruling of King Henry I that a road should be of sufficient width for six knights to ride abreast, the idea of traversing the B1222 as a day-long pedestrian odyssey is foolish indeed.

Instead, my thought was that you might like to dip into a book like this to enthuse you to go on a Sunday afternoon country drive. Or to take a rural bus ride. Or use a little-publicised rail service. Or to get pedalling along the cycleway.

However you get there, I mused you would have time to take in the features along the road, stop off for inspection of historic curios, and then assimilate it all at a suitable café or pub along the route.

## How to get there

Since this is a book about a road, the primary way of getting to the places mentioned is by using that road. What follows is a list of possible alternatives using public transport. The approximate timings and service intervals are those of Mon-Sat daytimes as in late 2020 but do check for updates online. Sunday services, if they exist, may be more sparse. The facilities listed are also as at late 2020 but are equally open to change. Please check before you set out.

I have mentioned 'official' parking places in the tour details, but several villages also have cafes and pubs as well as side streets. I will leave you to decide on the ethics of parking in such a way. If you do park up, ensure you do so with consideration for others.

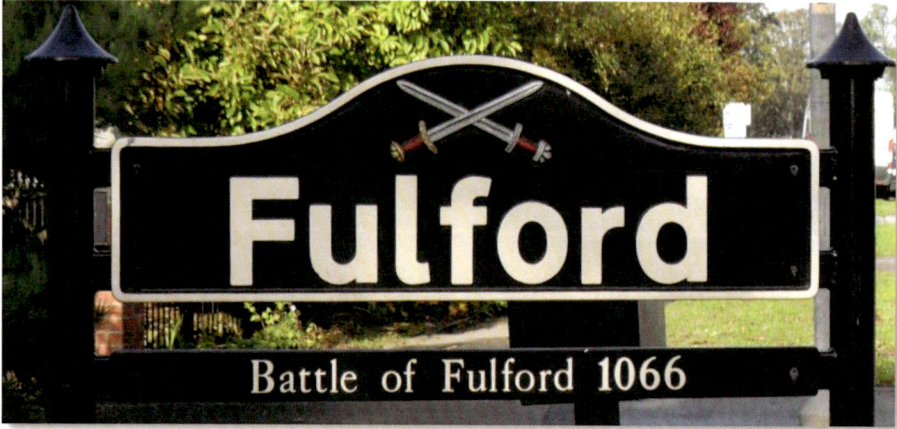

*The two 'ends of the road', - a phrase I'll refer to again - at the junction with the A19 at Fulford*

*and with the Great North Road (formerly the A1, now the A63) at South Milford.*

# Tour and transit details

## Tour 1 : Fulford

Arriva bus No. 42 every two hours from York or Selby. More regular service 415 from York City Centre and Selby Bus Station. Also the Designer Outlet Park and Ride service.

## Tour 2 : Designer Outlet

Arriva bus No. 42 every two hours from York or Selby, Mon - Sat, or No. 415 from York or Selby (every 15 minutes) and the Designer Centre Park and Ride service (every 10 minutes)

Toilets, shops and food outlets in Designer Centre.

Children's playground on site

## Tour 3 : Naburn

Arriva bus No. 42, every two hours from York or Selby, Mon - Sat.

Cycle along the Solar System cycleway.

Blacksmiths' Arms pub

## Tour 4 : Naburn Lock

Arriva bus No. 42, timings as above. River bus to and from York on some summer days.

Campsite shop

Parking and Tea rooms adjacent to lock site

## Tour 5 : Stillingfleet

Arriva bus No. 42, every two hours from York or Selby, Mon - Sat

Cross Keys pub (currently closed)

Garden, nursery and tea rooms.

## Tour 6 : Cawood

Arriva bus No. 42, every two hours from York or Selby, Mon - Sat.

Ferry Inn, Jolly Sailor and Castle pubs

Shop and café at Post Office. Garden centre

## Tour 7 : Bishopwood

No facilities. Free parking.

## Tour 8 : Sherburn in Elmet

No. 64 and 164 bus, hourly from Selby and Leeds

Irregular (approximately 2-hourly) train service from York or Selby or more occasionally from Pontefract

Several pubs

Small versions of supermarkets. Independent shops and cafés. Post Office and banks

## Transit 8

Food and drink and free parking at Squires' Café, Newthorpe.

## Tour 9 and 'End of the road' : Steeton Hall and the Great North Road

No facilities. There is free parking on the driveway in front of the Gateway, but please park with consideration for residents in the adjacent cottages. Please note that apart from the driveway and the exterior of the gateway, all else is private.

## A few other points

I have largely shied away from using geographic descriptors of directions. Instead, the entire journey is considered as being from Fulford to Milford, so references to items 'on the left' are to be read as if you are travelling in that direction. If you are travelling towards Fulford, you will need to reverse them.

If you are thinking of investigating the joys of the B1222 on a Wednesday evening or Sunday afternoon, do be aware that at those times there are often many bikers on the stretch of road between Stillingfleet and Newthorpe. This is not to imply that those on motor bikes are any better or any worse denizens of the highway than cyclists, motorists or lorry drivers. Just that at those times many bikers enjoy the B1222 as part of the 'Squires Coffee Bar' culture that has become part of local tradition. That tradition is covered in more detail in the section on Squires (page103).

There are four locations, Fulford; Naburn; Cawood and Sherburn, where more extensive walks are suggested, and I have produced sketch maps to help. These maps suggest a steady stroll but it is impossible to know quite what diversions and delights might take a visitor's fancy as they explore.

The length of each walk is no more than a mile, they could be comfortably done in under an hour and when researched in 2020 there seemed no major accessibility problems.

The descriptions "Bishopwood" and "Bishopdyke" occur repeatedly throughout the text. Different sources, of different antiquities, refer to these places in two words, sometimes both capitalised, sometimes not. I have attempted to keep to the forms above throughout. "Dyke" as a drainage channel is seen as both 'dyke' and 'dike' : I have used these interchangeably.

## Listed buildings

Some of the structures mentioned in the book are referred to as 'listed at Grade I' or similar. This refers to a list maintained by Historic England. There are three levels of 'listing', defined, in simple terms, as follows :

**Grade I** : buildings of exceptional interest.

**Grade II\*** : particularly important buildings of more than special interest.

**Grade II** : buildings that are of special interest, warranting every effort to preserve them.

To put those descriptions in context, local examples are : Grade I : York Minster; Grade II\* : York Theatre Royal and Grade II : York Art Gallery

## Common acronyms used

ECML : East Coast Main (railway) Line

C&RT : Canal and River Trust

SABRE : Society of British and Irish Road Enthusiasts

## Acknowledgements

Particular thanks to members and websites of local history societies based at Barwick in Elmet, Escrick, Naburn and Sherburn in Elmet; the Milestone Society, SABRE and South Milford Parish Council, for advice and the use of images and diagrams. After all that sage advice, any errors are mine and mine alone, and any opinions ventured are equally, solely my responsibly.

The images are all my own, unless noted otherwise. For these other images, I have not been able to contact all owners to request permission. If information is supplied, I will attribute the images accordingly in future editions.

Thanks to In-Print of Malton for printing and OCM design of Selby for the cover design

Thanks, of course, to my wife Mary and daughter Elspeth for encouragement, proof reading and unquenchable enthusiasm on visits to 'just one more little byway : it won't take long'.

# What's in a number : Why is the B1222 the B1222?

*Approaching the Low Street/Moor Lane junction from Moor Lane in Sherburn*

Here is one of the road signs at the main crossroads in Sherburn. Different colours, letters, numbers, brackets : what's that all about? The full story would, and does, take up many pages of several Department of Transport documents. For those interested, do study the site listed in the reference section. There is meaning in the seeming mumbo-jumbo, and it is worth a few pages to try to explain how our road got its number and what that number tells us.

## A brief history

England's first systematic road network was laid down by the Romans with their famous arrow-straight roads, such as Ermine Street (London to Lincoln and York) and the Fosse Way (linking Exeter and Lincoln). But these roads were never systematically numbered.

For the great majority of the population for the next millennium and a half, systematic road numbering system was irrelevant to their daily lives. Life was lived locally. Any long-distance traveller passing through in need of directions to a distant destination would probably be advised to '*follow yon track up the valley, over the hill and ask again when you get to the next village.*'

Many settlements had their 'London Road' which indicated the general direction towards one of the Roman arteries that would take you to the capital, but, beyond that, provided you knew which track took you to which local village, and the quickest way to the nearest market town, there was no need to know the name or number of the highway.

Meaningful and systematic designation of roads in modern England really only came to the fore with the advent of turnpike roads, established throughout the 18th and early 19th centuries. The story behind turnpikes is a long and detailed one, and extensive coverage is beyond the scope of this book.

In simple terms, turnpike roads were toll roads created between places of local significance, funded by local businessmen and landowners as a means of expediting trade by improving the conditions by which goods and people could move. 'Turnpike' referred to a barrier, of similar dimension to pikes used in battle, placed across the road adjacent to toll houses along the road. Examples of these toll cottages are still to be seen along many main roads that have taken over a former turnpike route.

Travellers could only have the barrier raised and be allowed to proceed on payment of the appropriate toll, depending on the nature of vehicle and the goods carried. A similar system still applies on the M6 Toll Road, the Tyne Tunnel or Humber Bridge in the UK today and commonly throughout Europe.

*Distance marker on the A63, formerly the Selby and Leeds turnpike, at Monk Fryston, 2019*

Once longer-distance journeys became more commonplace, it became more important to know which road you were on, or which road you needed to reach your destination. Turnpikes thus had localised signs and milestones that told you what turnpike road you were on and the distances to and from the nearest key towns. The Milestone Society are the people to consult f you need to know more on that score.

Sadly, as the 19th century progressed, the reputation of turnpikes began to sour. Some trusts were accused of being corrupt. Stopping at gates caused delay. Money was wasted. Some trusts ran up unsustainable debts. The coming of canals and then the railway brought fierce new competitors into the long-distance transport business.

## Local government steps in

From 1871, moves were made in Parliament to return roads to local administration, The Local Government Act of 1888 , which transferred powers to local authorities over such diverse matters as fish conservancy, race course licensing and lunatic asylums, also gave responsibility for maintaining main roads to county councils and county borough councils.

There were often great celebrations as the turnpikes were thrown open. The assets of the trust, such as tollhouses, gates and sections of surplus land beside the road were auctioned off to help defray any debt.

However, these local authorities did not find it easy to keep track of maintenance work. Traditionally, non-turnpike roads had been maintained by 'lengthsmen', a term dating back to Tudor times. In simple terms the men of the parish were responsible for the upkeep of the road, the quality of the drainage, the security of fencing and relevant boundary and direction marking as it passed through their parish. However, there were no common standards between different counties, so the state of a road could vary tremendously along its length. Similarly, signage was unreliable.

*An old-style County 'fingerpost' in North Wheatley, Nottinghamshire.*

So, in 1910, with the motor car making road journeys competitive and spurring improvement to the roads, action was taken to sort out the mess in England, Scotland and Wales. A government body called the Roads Board was set up under William Rees Jeffries, instructed to upgrade existing roads and build new ones using money from the new road and petrol tax.

## A system is born

The trouble Rees Jeffries and his colleagues faced was in working out just which roads should be funded, upgraded or replaced. There was nothing to tell them apart and no data available to say which roads were busy. In 1913, work began under Sir Henry Maybury, one of the Board's senior engineers. His principal concern was classification, categorising each road depending on how busy it was, to allow numbers to be allocated to each road for ease of reference.

To begin with, roads were said to be either Class I or Class II, but any numbering was restricted to individual counties, with the numbers confusingly changing at county boundaries.

Rather more pressing matters, in the form of the Great War in 1914 brought work to an abrupt stop. It was only in September 1919, as home affairs were returning to normal, that Sir Henry was invited to resume his classification work, now under the new Ministry of Transport.

As surveys of road usage came back in, maps were marked up to show which roads carried enough traffic or connected sufficiently important places to be regarded as Class I. The initial proposal was to use T (trunk) and L (link) for first and second class, but this was soon replaced by the idea of a simple A and B. The roads most used were awarded grade A, and the connecting roads deemed B. The designation was entirely down to levels of usage and made no comment on the size or state of the road.

Local authorities were encouraged to put numbers on new signs and to begin adding them to existing ones as soon as the first batch of numbers were made public in summer 1921. The Ministry of Transport covered all such costs, and once the first 99 A-roads were covered they were keen to see the signposting applied to progressively smaller and smaller routes.

The bones of the system were in place, now it was just a matter of sensibly fleshing them out.

The further evolution of the signage developed to inform motorists of the nature of the roads over which they were travelling and the destinations they could expect to reach is beyond the scope of this book. This evolution largely stems from the work of a committee under Sir Walter Worboys, that reported in 1963. An excellent discussion can be found in the "From War to Worboys" article on the roads.org.uk site.

## Hubs and spokes

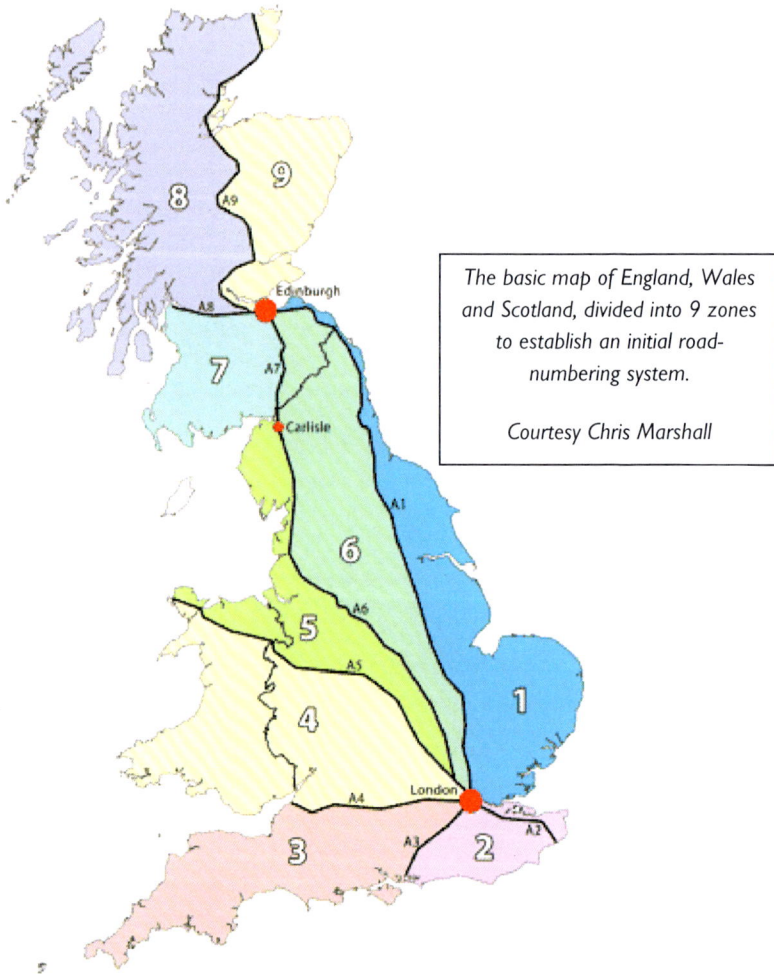

The basic map of England, Wales and Scotland, divided into 9 zones to establish an initial road-numbering system.

Courtesy Chris Marshall

The allocation of numbers is based on a 'hub-and-spoke' system. In its simplest form, this treats the City of London as the central point of the system, with all roads radiating out from it. As the map shows, this would lose some geographic utility in Scotland, as all roads would begin with a '6'. So, Edinburgh is deemed a second hub for the road system in Scotland.

Following on from this premise, there are six key radial roads in England, the A1 to the A6, and three more in Scotland, the A7, A8 and A9.

| Road no. | Start and finish locations |
|----------|---------------------------|
| A1 | London : Edinburgh |
| A2 | London : Dover |
| A3 | London : Portsmouth |
| A4 | London : Avonmouth |
| A5 | London : Holyhead |
| A6 | London : Carlisle |
| A7 | Edinburgh : Carlisle |
| A8 | Edinburgh : Greenock |
| A9 | Edinburgh : Scrabster (Orkney) |

These roads divide Great Britain into nine distinct areas. Each zone is numbered, taking its number from the A-road on its anticlockwise boundary. The exception to this rule is the boundary between zones 1 and 2, which is formed by the Thames Estuary and not the A2, in order to prevent a thin sliver of zone 1 being in the north of Kent.

From this point, the system is remarkably simple: other roads get their number according to which zone they lie in. Any road entirely contained in, say, zone 5 gets a number with the initial digit being a 5.

## Crossing the line

Just as the system counts upwards around its two hubs in a clockwise direction, a decision was made in 1922 that all other roads travel around the country in a clockwise direction. But that brings a potential problem if a road traverses two or more different zones.

A further 1922 rule decreed every road started at its "furthest anticlockwise terminus".

In the theoretical example in the diagram, a road lies across two zones, numbers 4 and 5. From a London point of view zone 4 is 'more anticlockwise' than zone 5, so this road would be given a number starting '4'.

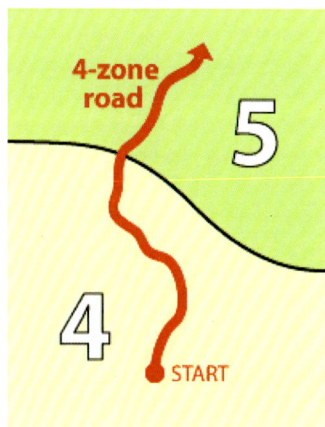

'Crossing the line' diagram
Courtesy Chris Marshall

To apply this rule to a real example, consider the A road that, in its original routing, ran from just east of Bath to just west of Grimsby. Following that route on the map, it passes through zone 4, then 5 then 6 and ends in 1. If you think of the hands of the clock spreading out from London, then the most anticlockwise of these zones is number 4. The road was therefore given a number starting with 4, and, in reality, is the A46. Although the route has changed a little recently, the argument, and road number, still applies.

Since a few roads may have special or historic antecedents, these rules don't always hold, but from the two basic ideas of the spokes and the clockface, the numbers given for the vast majority of A roads can be explained.

### What about the spokes that come off the spokes?

Once the initial digit of the key radial roads has been determined, numbers for roads that branch off these spokes are allocated equally logically. Again, allowing for the fact that there are exceptions that disprove the general rule, usually speaking, the more important the road, the shorter its number. A-roads can have one, two, three or four digits. When we come to B-roads, their designations are either three- or four-digit ones..

So, the next phase of applying the rules gave lower numbers to branching spokes nearer the hub. The example of Zone 1, main roads radiating from the A1, shows this nicely.

| Road number | Start and finish locations |
|---|---|
| A10 | London : Norwich |
| A11 | London : Kings Lynn |
| A12 | London : Great Yarmouth |
| A13 | London : Southend |
| A14 | Rugby : Felixstowe |
| A15 | Peterborough : Hull |
| A16 | Stamford : Grimsby |
| A17 | Newark : Kings Lynn |
| A18 | Doncaster : Grimsby |
| A19 | Doncaster: Newcastle |

This is the numbering that would happen in an ideal world, where roads were never altered, diverted or constructed. Creation of new roads or by passes that fit in between these original numberings and the introduction of 4-figure A roads have meant the hub-and-spoke procedure has had to be modified somewhat, but the basic premise still applies.

New road building and upgrading to motorway status does sometimes mean the original letter or number of a road 'disappears' for a stretch, but the terminal destination remains as it was originally.

Three-digit road numbers for A roads get their numbers in batches. Again, lower numbers are nearer the hub and higher numbers are further away. So, in zone 4, A400 to A409 are in central and west London; A440 to A449 are in Worcestershire; A480 to A489 run across west Wales.

## What about the B's?

As referred to earlier, B roads were originally those with lower traffic densities than the main trunk, or A roads. Their purpose as 'link' roads is to move traffic to and from the more major roads. The prefix B implies nothing about the width or quality of the road, so their quality can range all the way from dual carriageways to single track roads with passing places. It is how much traffic uses the road, not the quality of the road that makes a 'B' a 'B'.

## And the B1222 itself?

At last, we can turn to the subject of the book : the B1222. How did it come by its number?

The B meant that, in the surveys of the 1920s, the road carried comparatively little traffic. East to west travel across this part of Yorkshire was more conveniently done by the A64 (Leeds-Scarborough) or the A19/A63 (Doncaster- Selby - Hull) combination. The job of the B1222 as a link road was to allow traffic from the villages along its route to connect to two major routes, the York to Doncaster A19 and the A1/Great North Road which ultimately links London and Edinburgh, and to provide a secondary route if either of the A roads were blocked.

Geographically, the B1222 lies entirely within zone 1, being seen as starting at the A1, the western boundary of the '1's', so its number begins with 1.

The second digit of a batch of B's depends on distance from London. In general, the closer to the hub of London, the lower the second digit.

By and large, the B1000 family are to be found in and around Suffolk and Essex, the B1100s around Cambridgeshire, Norfolk and Lincolnshire. The B1200s stretch from Louth in Lincolnshire as far north as South Shields. The final two numbers should - in an ideal world - anchor the road in a specific geographical area. However, the system isn't always perfect!

Our B1222's close family - the B1220s - is a diverse one, mostly, but not entirely, traversing the southern hinterland of York. The 1222, as already noted is Fulford to the Great North Road. The 1223 links Selby to Towton, and crosses the 1222 in Cawood. The 1224 is the Wetherby to York road and the 1228 joins York to Boothferry near Howden. So far so sensible.

Yet some others in the 1220 family have gone a long way from this York-based 'home'. The B1220 does the same job as the 1222 in linking the Great North Road to the A19 but on merely a 5-mile run, and much further south, starting at Skellow just north of Doncaster. The 1225 is in Lincolnshire, between Horncastle and Caistor. The 1229 is permanently on vacation on Yorkshire's East Coast between Reighton to Flamborough.

Wherever they are, at least those roads are highways of reasonable distance, in contrast, the B1221, 1226 and 1227 are remarkably short lengths of road.

The 1221 used to be a road around a half a mile long connecting Knottingley to Ferrybridge, but it became renumbered as the B6136. The number was then transferred to Middlesbrough where it now describes an equally short length of tarmac in Ormesby that used to be part of the A171.

The 1226 is the designation given to less than a mile of the former A15/Ermine Street near Lincoln, when it was downgraded, and the 1227 covers the short distance from Rougier Street to Tower Street in York.

In each case there will have been a logical reason for the designation of such stretches as distributor roads. This discussion may already have seemed quite convoluted, but for those fascinated by the system and wishing to explore the machinations of the Men from the Ministry and their numbering further, the websites in the reference section are recommended.

## What about the colours and the brackets?

Before we finish, we need to return to the sign that began this section. Its design and varied colours are equally the result of the application of a series of logical rules.

The sign has black lettering on a white background, because it is on a B road, and that is the colour scheme for B roads. But to go to Leeds you need an A road, so the A63 is yellow on green because that's the colour scheme for A roads. The A63 is in brackets, because it is a branch off the B1222, not directly on it. The sign is telling you *'if you keep going along the B1222 you'll get to a junction where you can branch off onto the A63'*. The purpose of the brackets is to tell the motorist that such branching awaits.

But then you notice that the A162 to Tadcaster and Ferrybridge is in black and white, not green and yellow. That is because as roads have become more complex, the A road category has been split into 'primary' and 'non primary' routes. The A63 is deemed primary, so gets green and yellow. The A162 deemed 'non primary' even though it's an A, so it is in black. Sounds complex, but really just a tweaking of the 'traffic density' plan from 1922. Since the photo was taken, Low Street has been further downgraded : the 'A162' is now covered up.

For similar reasons, the A1 is in brackets and in white on blue, because those are the motorway colours. The brackets around the 'M' have a different meaning. They are passing on the information that the A1 is an A road uprated to a motorway and not a 'true' motorway!

Finally, the 'inferior' status of B roads is demonstrated because, whilst putting a green/yellow primary route patch on a black and white secondary route sign is allowed, you can't put a black/white secondary route sign on a primary one. So a secondary route on a primary route sign can be in yellow - as the indication of the B1222 on the sign on page 26 shows.

Oh, and the font itself is planned for the purpose too! Designers Jock Kinnear and Margaret Calvert created a special typeface called 'Transport' intended for easy legibility when travelling at speed. This was introduced to signs in the UK during the 1960s, replacing the Maybury signs and unregulated styles on County fingerposts and turnpike milestones.

In this section, I hope I have been concise yet comprehensive. Should you wish to research further, do consult the websites and the DfT manual in the reference section. But enough theory! It is certainly time now to explore the road and the history and geography it traverses.

Standardised signage at the junction with the old A1, approaching the junction in Cawood and an entirely non-standard, but entirely appropriate fingerpost at Moor Lane in Naburn.

# Tour 1 : The battle of Fulford

*A medieval tapestry depicting the Battle of Fulford,*
*Professor Chas. Jones explaining about the battle on site in the 950th anniversary year of 2016.*

This book is all about a road with a number :1222. But before we follow its story, we need to consider a number with an even greater relevance to English history: 1066. We all know what happened in that year. An Anglo-Saxon king. An arrow in the eye. The start of the Norman Conquest.

You would be right. But you would also be wrong. The Battle of Hastings was merely the culmination of the tumultuous autumn of 1066 that featured three battles that changed the course of the nation that we now know as England forever.

The second of those battles was at Stamford Bridge in East Yorkshire, but the first was at Fulford. So, on the very site where our road begins, the destiny of our nation began to change over 950 years ago.

On January 6th of that fateful year, England's long-ruling and pious king Edward the Confessor died. His piety was undoubted, but this piety was such that he failed to consummate his marriage and so had committed the cardinal sin for a medieval monarch of dying without leaving an obvious heir. Harold Godwinson, who, at the time, was effectively a well-placed warlord, claimed the throne. Sadly, for old England, many other dukes and kings across Europe had equally valid claims and wasted no time in preparing to press them.

We know who the ultimate winner was. The Norman, William, eventually succeeded at Hastings, but his victory is only a sideshow to our story here. Kings in the Scandinavian regions also had claims on the English throne. Danish King Cnut, perhaps better known as Canute, had ruled England as part of the Danish empire from the year 1016, and his sons briefly followed until the last one died in 1042 when Edward took the throne. So, the idea of a Scandinavian ruling England was still within living memory. With that knowledge, Norwegian King Harald Hardrada set forth to make his claim.

With a force of 300 ships, meaning possibly 7 or 8000 men, Hardrada set off in the late summer of 1066. After enjoying some plundering and raiding along the coast, the fleet sailed up the Humber and into the Ouse, eventually mooring near Riccall, about 10 miles, or 3 hours' march, south of York.

The year had now turned and it was mid-September. This meant that it was close to the autumn equinox, when tides are at the strongest. Following the building of lock and weir at Naburn, the Ouse ceased to be tidal at York. But, back in 1066, tidal flows affected the level of the river in the Fulford area . An increase in the Ouse's depth of two feet or so was entirely possible around an equinox. With Fulford's battle taking place close to water courses, on low lying and potentially marshy land, such tides would have a crucial part to play in the battle.

On the early morning of September 20th, leaving behind a contingent to guard their ships, several thousand Norse warriors set out to march to the regional centre of government at York. The Anglo Saxons based in York were not unaware of the threat. They could have stayed defensively behind the city's walls but decided to march out to meet the invaders with a view to repelling them whence they came. The Anglo Saxon forces were under the leadership of Earl Morcar of Northumbria and Earl Edwin of Mercia. In modern terms, the forces of the midlands and north of England were ready to do battle.

To that end, they marched the two miles south to what we now know as Fulford, but back then was a series of unconnected hamlets including 'Gate Fulford' and 'Water Fulford' amongst others.

The etymology of 'Fulford' suggests it could derive from 'Foul Ford': a muddy crossing of a shallow waterway. This waterway to be forded was not the Ouse, but Germany Beck - a stream that ran into the Ouse at Fulford, and is still extant today, having recently been re-channelled under the main A19 road The nearby modern 'Fordlands Road' hints at the former nature of the local environment. The Beck made its marshy and meandering way into the Ouse across Fulford Ings. In early autumn, it is not unreasonable to suggest most of the area was, at best, damp underfoot.

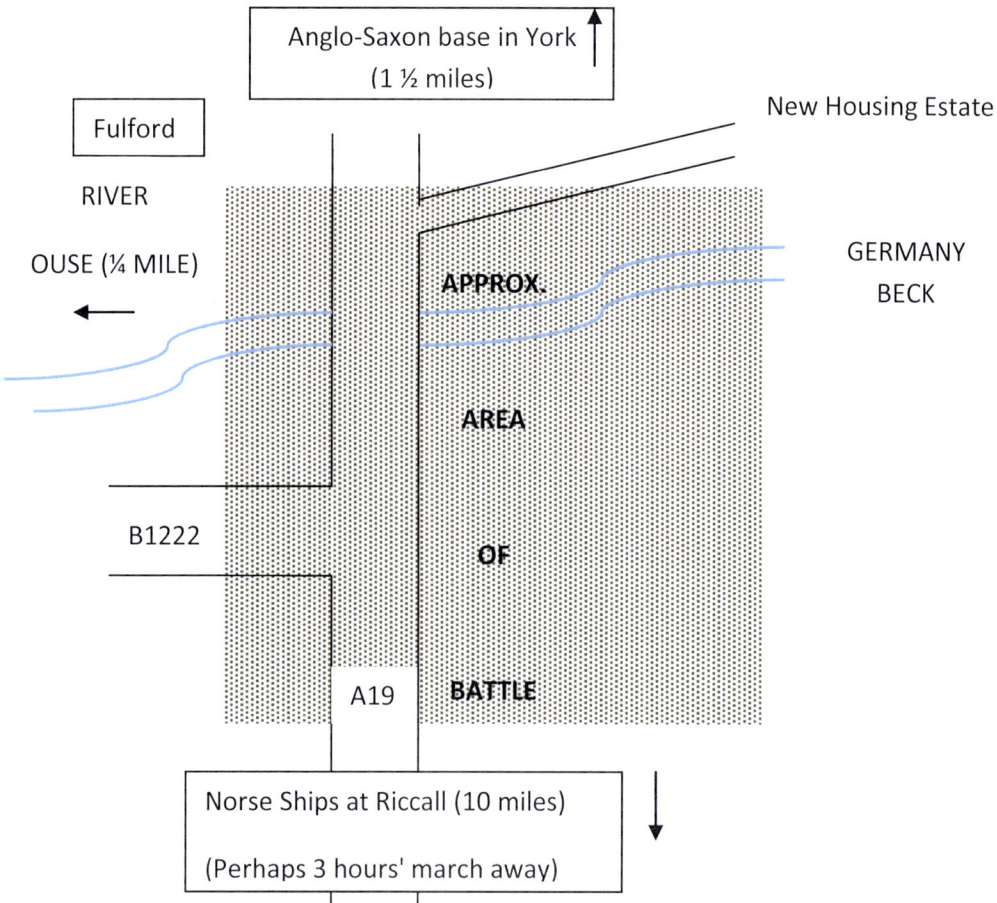

At that early hour in the morning an incoming tide on the Ouse was pushing water up the beck, making it now perhaps 30 feet wide. The Anglo Saxon forces prepared on the north bank of the beck, with Morcar more 'inland' and Edwin closer to the Ouse. With some 4-5 000 men at their command, a wall of warriors, several deep would have stretched for some distance along the bank. However, the position was not without its disadvantages. With marshy land to one side and the Ouse to the other, escape to either flank would be difficult. Furthermore, the land to the south was higher than that to the north, giving the invading forces a better overview of the battleground.

*Germany Beck in October 2020: placidly flowing across Fulford Ings, adjacent to the B1222. Its confluence with the Ouse is perhaps 100 yards away, by the distant tree line.*

As the morning progressed, Norse forces gradually arrived on the southern bank. Whilst the tide was up, the opposing forces could do little more than glare at each other, but around noon, the tide had abated sufficiently to encourage Morcar to advance and engage Hardrada's men. Initially Morcar was successful and pushed Hardrada's men back, crossing the beck.

The arrival of further, fresher Norsemen swung the battle. Attacking Edwin across the ford close to the river, Harald's forces overcame them and pushed round, coming onto Morcar's forces from the rear. Morcar's men were now in a terrible position. They had not been able to cut through Harald's lines at the front, were being assailed from the rear and fatally hemmed in at the flanks by the marsh and the Ouse. Nothing was left but to fight to the end.

Whilst some managed to escape back to York, for many their end was indeed in Fulford's fields. So many ended their days there that it is said the Norsemen were able to walk off the battlefield dry-shod over the bodies of the fallen.

The subsequent events : Harold's magnificent march to defeat the Norsemen at Stamford Bridge, and his doomed attempt to do the same to the Normans at Hastings are beyond the scope of this book.

On the ground today there is little to mark the site of the carnage. For much of the 20th. century the area was largely overgrown scrubland with Germany Beck innocently pootling on its way, apart from times of flood when it would block the A19 south of York. A controversial new housing estate where earth-moving began shortly after the 950th anniversary of the battle has effectively sterilised much of the site from further investigation and markers attached to road signs are the only easily-visible reminders of the conflict. A small memorial cairn may still exist on site.  To inspect the area around the beck, take one of the paths shown on the sketch map here. Either follow Landing Lane, beyond a height-bar off the A19, take the path across fields, or follow the stub of the B1222 on the right just beyond the junction. The ground may well be - as in September 1066 - damp underfoot, but is ideal for a creature as endangered as a Saxon warrior : the tansy beetle. Access from St. Oswald's Court is down a tricky slope.

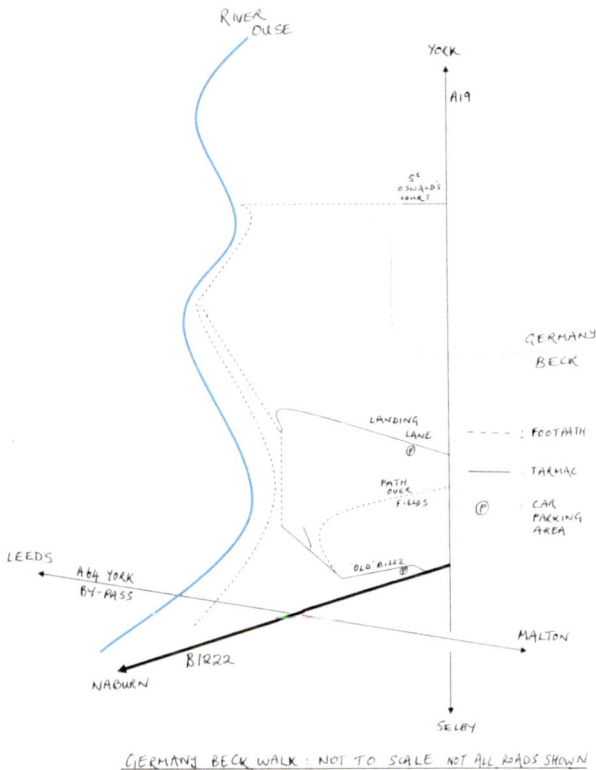

GERMANY BECK WALK : NOT TO SCALE  NOT ALL ROADS SHOWN

*Tansy beetle board close to the confluence of Germany Beck and River Ouse.*

It is now appropriate to follow the arrows of a road sign rather than those loosed on a battlefield, as the B1222 begins its link-road task of forging a route between fields where perhaps five thousand fighters fell in the first of the three tumultuous battles of September 1066 and the great north-south highway of England, used by millions over the years.

*An invitation to begin the journey : the A19/B1222 junction in Fulford*

*Leaving behind the site of the battle : the B1222/A19 junction.*

Following the bidding of the sign pictured at the bottom of page 26, turn right across the busy A19 to the quieter carriageway of the B1222. In that sense, the designations of a century ago still hold true. On this section of its journey, the B1222 takes on the first of its many 'local names' : in this case 'Naburn Lane'. The blue warning sign in the distance advises of limited clearance under a bridge at Naburn, and weight restrictions over the bridge at Cawood.

***To save frustration and three-point turns, please read the section in italics on the next page first before setting off if you want to visit the Designer Outlet by car.***

Having left the site of the battle and begun our journey, almost at once the first interruption to the original line of the road comes into view. Until the mid-1970s, the road continued along a flat and sinuous course, to be seen off to the right of the current roadway. You can now park up on this part of it, with traces of white lines still visible, over 40 years after it ceased to be a through route. If you park here you can follow a path across the Ings back to the A19, as mentioned on page 25. One 1970s lamp standard remains at a corner, hidden in a bush.

This open land hereabouts was part of the original Fulford Golf Course. One of the Naburn Lane houses bears the name 'Old Links House' : a reminder of these previous times. The new B1222 now swoops over the York Outer Ring Road whose development caused the deviation. Make sure you swoop at no more than 30mph. On the left is a series of low walls and beech hedging that has been allowed to grow into full-sized trees. These are the remains of the front walls, gates and hedges of houses for staff who used to work at the hospitals that were once on the site of the Designer Outlet. There is more about them in 'Tour 2'.

To the left, behind a fine belt of shelter trees lies the McArthur Glen Shopping Outlet, which was constructed and opened in 1998 on the site of the former Naburn and Fulford Hospitals. Given the history of York and the closeness of the site of the battle, an archaeological survey was carried out on site prior to construction, but nothing of significance was found.

If you have come by bus or bike to visit the Outlet, enter here via the 'emergency gate'. The avenue of trees marked the original entrance to the hospital site.

*The Designer Outlet from the A64 bridge, nicely shielded by a fine shelter belt of trees*

*If driving, note there is no car access from the B1222 to the Outlet and no reasonable roadside parking. The Outlet has free parking, so to follow tour 2, <u>do not drive down Naburn Lane</u>, but continue along the A19 to the major roundabouts. Follow the signs to the Designer Outlet. As you enter the Outlet's system, take the right-hand lane. Bear right with the main buildings on your left and park. The walking route from Naburn Lane eventually merges into this car park area.*

# Tour 2 : Naburn's Hospitals and Shops

Almost as soon as the new course of the B1222 rejoins the old one, as noted on the previous page, on the left is what has become a major shopping attraction for residents of York and visitors alike, the McArthur Glen Designer Outlet.

*Looking back to the bridge over the A64 : original course of the B1222 to the left*

However, before the shops came, for almost a century the site was home to maternity and mental hospitals. Very little remains of these buildings, so in terms of a 'tour' this is largely a discussion of the history of the site. The 'tour' - unless you go shopping - is limited to a visit to the old hospital orchard. However, as the hospitals did once play a crucial part in the lives of many Yorkies, as the commercial activities now do, what has occupied this site deserves consideration. What has replaced them is very much an example of modern 'history', so some shopping can also count as historical exploration.

The Hospitals

There were actually three separate medical facilities on the Naburn site, Naburn Asylum or Mental Hospital, Fulford Hospital and the Maternity Hospital ; each have their own history..

To start with the Asylum. Back in 1845, the Lunacy Act was passed, which gave York Corporation responsibility for people said to be 'pauper lunatics'. Despite pressure from the Care Quality Commission of its time - the wonderfully-entitled 'Commissioners for Lunacy' - it was 60 years before York properly discharged its responsibility by opening what was called the York Asylum at Naburn in 1906.

In 1899 the City purchased 140 acres of land and the buildings of Acres House Farm to build the asylum. City Surveyor Alfred Creer designed a fine building. As the aerial picture from between the World Wars shows, the hospital complex was not a modest affair. Approached from Naburn Lane where a gate and lodge protected access to the grounds via a fine, tree-lined avenue.

Cottages were built to accommodate married attendants and their families, a large, detached chapel and an administration block. To the east stood the maintenance yard, boiler house, workshops and mortuary. Other buildings included a laundry, sewing room and drying grounds, stores, delivery yard, kitchens and recreation and dining hall, and a residence for the Assistant Medical Officer. From personal experience, I can report there was a fine cricket pavilion and ground, too.

*Aerial view of the hospitals at Naburn, possibly 1930s (unknown). The B1222 is mid-left to top right*

On the picture, Naburn Lane runs between hospital and river. Between the lane and the river is the former clubhouse of Fulford Golf Club. The garden walls of the properties facing Naburn Lane remain, as referred to on page 28, underneath dense undergrowth. The tree-lined avenue from Naburn Lane is still partially in place, but all the buildings have gone. Mature trees that are to be found around the Outlet's buildings were once part of the hospital's grounds.

The central clock, built by York-based clockmaker George Newey, atop a water tower, was a distinctive local landmark,. When the site was cleared for the Outlet, the four faces and mechanism were removed and are said to be in store awaiting a new home. The bell from the water tower, by John Taylor & Co. of Loughborough, also survived and is now part of a peal of eight at All Saints' , Helmsley.

After opening in 1906, the asylum seems to have settled down to do a thoroughly satisfactory job, with 6 male and 6 female wards, with a total capacity eventually reaching 486 patients. Occasional staff shortages did cause some problems, but by and large the patients had a wide range of worthwhile tasks to take part in. An early report described the patients as being *"kindly and considerately treated"*. Steady progress and improvements were made throughout the 1920s and 30s, but the start of World War 2 brought changes.

The War Department took over two wards, but, more importantly, developed the empty northern part of the site and formed what is described as a 'hutted hospital'. Whilst the wards in the asylum were returned to their original use in 1942, the huts stayed with the War Dept. In 1947 they were used to house Prisoners of War, but later that decade they were returned to the newly-formed NHS, and over the course of the next few years became the Fulford and Maternity Hospitals.

The Fulford Hospital opened in October 1954, with wards for gynaecology, dermatology and geriatrics, serving 149 patients in all. There were two operating theatres, a range of medical services and accommodation for up to 100 staff. The Maternity Hospital had beds for 108 women with the expected range of ante- and post-natal services as well as delivery rooms. It was also a centre for the training of midwives.

*Maternity Hospital Entrance (courtesy naburnvillage.org)*

Meanwhile, in 1948, the Asylum had been renamed 'Naburn Hospital' and a report in the same year described it as a *'happy hospital'* with patients who were *'remarkably contented'*. In 1952 it formally joined with Bootham Park Hospital.

Steady progress, development and introduction of new ideas and machinery continued in all three hospitals throughout the 1960s, including a GP unit in 1965 at the Maternity hospital. Such progress continued into the early 1970s.

However, new ways of caring for people with mental health problems were being developed, and services began to be centralised in York. The hutted hospital buildings were also starting to show their age. Fulford's dermatology and gynaecological departments closed in December 1976, with geriatrics following in May 1979. The buildings remained open for temporary or emergency use until June 1983.

The Maternity hospital gradually transferred its treatments and patients to the new facilities at York District Hospital, with final closure being in December 1983.

A similar decline took place at the mental hospital. Gradual closure of wards and transfer of patients to more central and modern facilities in York led to final closure in February 1988.

*The Hospital Gatehouse on Naburn Lane, as site clearance began, late 1980s.*

The hospital buildings and site were cleared soon after closure to eventually become the Outlet and car parking, and effectively no structures from either the asylum buildings or hutted complex remain. Some farm buildings still survive at the original Acres House site, as well as the housing opposite the hospital's main gate, all now private houses. The major survivors from the medical era are the mature trees dotted around the site, and a remnant of the hospital orchard to the side of the approach road from the main road to the car park.

## The Orchard

Walk to the 'top end' of the car park beyond the playground and cross the access road, following signs to Fulford Community Orchard. This is part of the one acre orchard in the six acre Kitchen Garden which provided fruit and vegetables for the staff and patients of Naburn Hospital from 1906 until possibly the early 1960s. At least 50 varieties of apple, damson, pear and plum trees survive from a century ago, along with newer trees planted to make up for gaps that have arisen over 60 years of neglect. The Orchard is free to visit. A notice board by the entrance gives further detail of activities of the volunteers now in charge of the site.

*Fulford Community Orchard : a newly-cherished remnant of Naburn Hospital's more extensive orchard*

## McArthur Glen Shopping Outlet

Although it may seem odd to think of a shopping centre as part of a historical narrative, but as the Outlet has been in business since 1988, it has become part of York's story. Since the B1222 forms part of the boundary of the site, it forms part of the road's story too. It also is a historical marker of the late 1980s when many similar centres opened throughout the nation. Developments such as Meadowhall near Sheffield and Bluewater to the east of London were the new, bright face of shopping.

Free parking, shops under cover in clean and air conditioned surroundings; the attraction compared to the fuddy-duddy High Street was obvious. McArthur Glen at Naburn was never in that league, but with a wide range of shops, offering goods at greatly reduced prices, places to eat and a free children's play area as well, the draw was strong.

The late 1980s were also a time when the phrase 'Designer Fashion' came into vogue. It was no longer good enough to have well-made and smartly-fitting clothes. It was equally important to have the most 'hip and happening' fashionable label or logo displayed. In High Street shops, these garments would be offered for crazily inflated prices. After a few weeks, the clothes would be moved to the retail outlet at Naburn at greatly reduced (some might say normal) prices.

This arrangement led to the description 'Designer Outlet' by which it is commonly known today.

Arguments over whether the new Outlet affected shopping in York's centre continue to rage. There was also controversy as what was once a dark and often misty evening location, with associated wildlife, became glitzy and bright with garish street lighting. This was subsequently toned down, and the problem largely solved.

*Viking Boat at Designer Outlet  (courtesy Andy Farrington/Geograph)*

The architects paid homage to the Viking history linked to the Battle of Fulford by creating an impressive model Viking boat that was suspended from the ceiling in one of the café areas.

Sadly, the craft, like its Viking forebears, are no longer present on site. Leaving aside any judgement on 'Outlet' shopping, the site is a fine place to visit, especially to appreciate the specimen mature trees that remain from the original hospital.

It is now time to return to the B1222. If you are catching the bus or using a bike, return along the splendid avenue of trees to Naburn Lane. For bus travellers, the bus stop and shelter are just by the remnants of the garden walls.

Across the road, the York-bound sanctuary is a fine example of rural outpost and post-box combined. For cyclists the use of a few hundred yards of cycle track on the far side of the road is recommended.

For motorists, from the car park, return to the A19, follow directions to York at the roundabouts and turn left onto the B1222 just after the 'Battle of Fulford ' signs. Up and over the A64 and the Designer Outlet is to the left.  Bitter experience reminds me to remind you once more to beware of the speed limit !

*Always a pleasure to meet a team-mate of Lewis Hamilton, sir.*
*Perhaps sir could press a little more gently with the right foot next time.*

# Transit 2 : Designer Outlet to Naburn Village

The next stretch of the B1222, is brief : less than a mile to the attractions in and around Naburn village.

Through the hedge to the left you might just be able to glimpse some of the buildings that make up Acres Farm: the farm to which the land that is now occupied by the Designer Outlet once belonged. However, soon a development to the right threatens to kick up a stink!

## Naburn Waste Water Treatment Works

Each day , the population of the south-west part of York sends out enough waste water to fill over 40 Olympic swimming pools (or more scientifically, 2.5 million litres or 500 000 gallons). This comes to York's sewerage treatment works in Naburn.

According to a recent newspaper article, the 'raw material' arrives in four separate pipelines, from Fulford, the University, the Designer Outlet and Bishopthorpe. Just over a day later the cleaned water is returned to the Ouse. Unfortunately, on one occasion things didn't go to plan, In 2013 a stretch of river around a kilometre was affected by sewage discharge after a pump failed.

But when all is working well, treatment of the waste produces methane which is used to generate electricity to power the site's equipment. The plant was initially constructed in 1895 at a cost of £165,000, about £14 million in today's values

The sludge left after the water is cleaned and filtered is donated to local farmers to compost their fields. Originally the works had its own internal railway line to transport sludge around the site. The wagons were once pulled by horses and carts but later a small locomotive was employed. In 1989, some of the sludge trucks were transferred to the Ripon & District Light Railway.

The works are screened from the road by a row of conifers, but however much you are a fan of the natural cycles, it is still advisable to close the car windows as one drives by.

*Former Naburn Works' Sewage Sludge Trucks (courtesy Ripon & District Light Railway)*

*A welcoming sign at the entrance to a historic riverside village*

Moving on swiftly past the sewage works, directly ahead is a simple metal girder bridge across the road. For over a century this carried the East Coast Main Line (ECML) : Flying Scotsman, Mallard and all the other famous locomotives crossed here. Naburn village lies just ahead, and if you are stopping to do this tour, it is probably best to go ahead, park up, and then walk back to take it all in.

There is the general village ambience, the scene around the river and the development of former railway line that crossed the B1222 and River Ouse, all to absorb. Naburn is recorded as a settlement before the Norman Conquest, and is also mentioned in the Domesday Book. Various families held the manor over the next 150 years or so, until William Palmes gained the estate in 1226. The family remained in control, at Naburn Hall, until the death of the final member of the line in 1974. Palmes Court in the centre of the village commemorates this 750-year-long tenure.

Assuming you have parked up in the village, the map and accompanying descriptions on the following pages will give you a pleasant stroll around this riverside village

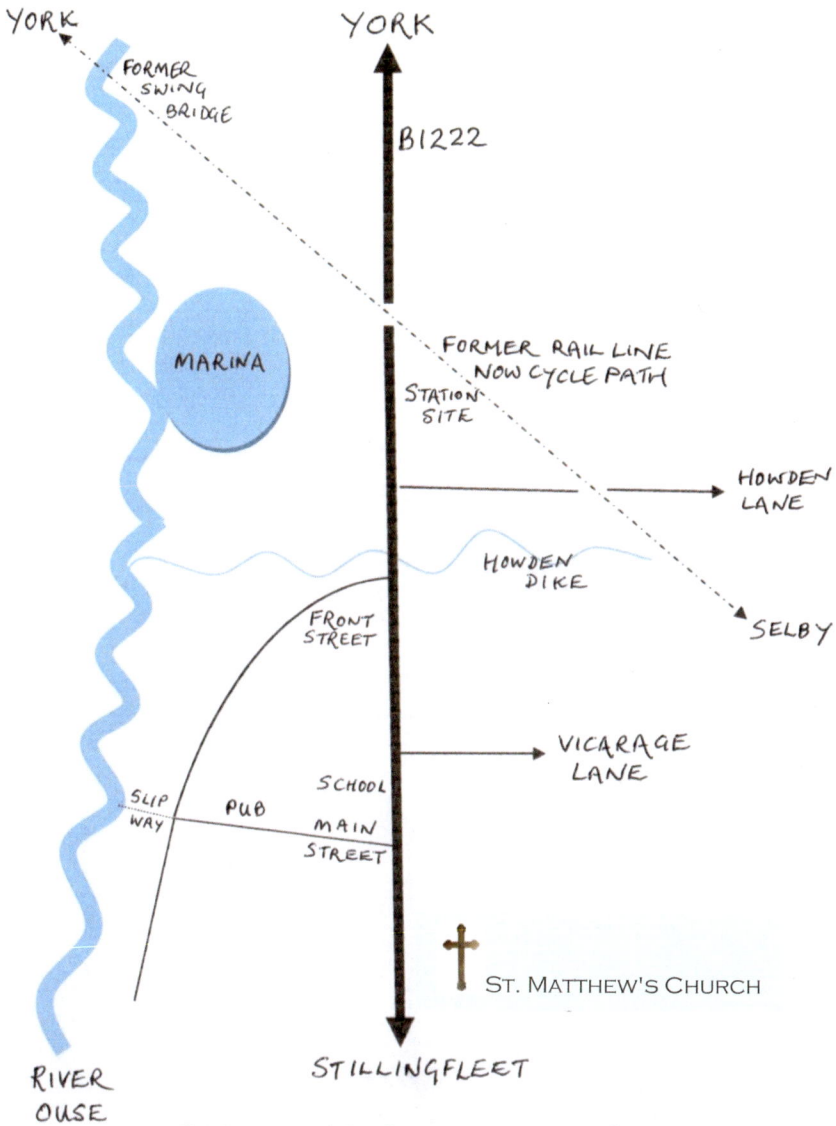

YORK

FORMER SWING BRIDGE

YORK

B1222

MARINA

FORMER RAIL LINE NOW CYCLE PATH

STATION SITE

HOWDEN LANE

HOWDEN DIKE

SELBY

FRONT STREET

VICARAGE LANE

SLIP WAY

PUB

SCHOOL

MAIN STREET

St. Matthew's Church

STILLINGFLEET

RIVER OUSE

SKETCH MAP for NABURN WALK

NOT TO SCALE : NOT ALL ROADS SHOWN

Walk back from the village towards the former railway line, on the right-hand side of the road, pass under the bridge and follow a curved path up onto the former railway line. This is now a cycleway and footpath. However the closure of Naburn's village station didn't follow the usual unhappy tale of a 'Beeching closure'.

Naburn railway station was on the original ECML, an intermediate station between Selby and York, along with stations at Escrick and Riccall. Whilst over a hundred trains a day thundered through Naburn, across both the road bridge as well as the rather more interesting River Ouse swing bridge a hundred yards or so towards York, very few actually stopped to serve the population. Generally there were only three services each way, Monday to Saturday. A morning train to get you to work or school, a matching one at the end of the working day and a third around lunchtime. No service on the Sabbath, naturally.

Naburn station opened in 1871. With such service, it is a surprise that it remained open for passengers until June 1953. But that is probably putting a modern spin on what is expected of a railway and what kind of place Naburn is. Nowadays, many Naburn residents either commute to or shop in York. The thought of a 10-minute journey into the heart of town sounds great. But that is on a nippy modern commuter unit that can accelerate quickly. Back in 1952 this service probably comprised a few ancient carriages pulled by an equally venerable loco.

What's more, the ECML only had two tracks here and the amount of time it would have taken a local, stopping service to slow down and restart would have delayed the much more important expresses. Local trains could only be fitted in in lengthy gaps between expresses.

Also, seventy years ago, a village provided much more in the way of work and goods to purchase. It is therefore reasonable to think that the loss of the service was not felt too badly. However, rail was still seen as important for the movements of freight, as the goods service only ceased in 1964. Such freight might have been coal for domestic use, for the village gas works, or agricultural produce being sent to market. This need would have been met via sidings that abutted and also to the side of the station buildings

The ECML continued to run through Naburn until it was diverted away from Selby in 1983 as will be described in the section on the Selby Coalfield.

Fairly soon after the new Selby Diversion came into operation in October 1983, track was removed from the former line. The southern part of the route between Riccall and Selby became a new course for the A19 road. Transport charity Sustrans was allowed to buy the remaining trackbed from Riccall to the south-west outskirts of York for £1 to form a cycleway as part of the National Cycle Network. It became a section of Route 65 of the Network linking Hornsea to Middlesbrough with this section joining the ferry terminal at Hull with Selby and York.

Naburn Station.

Above : Naburn Station mid 1930s (naburnvillage.org) . Below : A1 4-6-2 60135 'Madge Wildfire' thunders south through Naburn, April 1962. Note the sidings to the left. (courtesy David Holmes)

*Naburn Station Site, 2015*

Having considered the history, what remains on site today? The station itself, now a private residence, remains, as does the York-bound platform in front of it. The small goods yard with three sidings was behind the house, but nothing of this can now be seen from the path.

Walking past the station site, there is an area put aside for seats, information and sometimes snacks. Going a little further in this direction is a viewing mound which allows - on a good day - a sight of York Minster. Just beyond this is a very stylish metal bridge over Howden Lane, after which the path opens out into countryside on the way to Riccall.

Returning to the station site, a model of the Cassini/Huygens probe built by the European Space Agency stands in the same area as the signal post did in the old pictures. This may seem an exceedingly odd structure to find in rural North Yorkshire, but there is method in the seeming madness. After Sustrans had built and established the cycle route, scientists from the University of York got involved. They decided to lay out a scale model of the Solar System to fit the length of the path between York and Riccall. The scale is apparently 575,872,239 to 1. The installation of this monster-scale set of models allowed the promoters to encourage cyclists, walkers and pedestrians to imagine their exercise as a voyage through the Solar System. Many enthusiastic would-be cosmonauts and astronauts undertake the expedition,

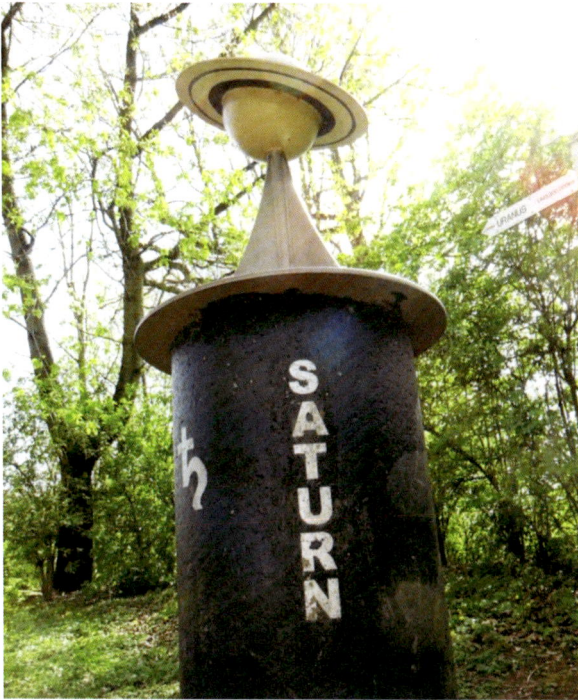

*The Saturn marker point and spacecraft model, adjacent to Naburn's former station*

Continue along the path, and, to the left, you can see the large number of boats moored up at the marina. In the middle distance a metallic structure looms. This is Naburn Swing Bridge.

*A northbound passenger service crosses at Naburn, 1950s (courtesy naburnvillage.org)*

*The 'Fisher of Dreams' perching on the Naburn Swing Bridge structure*

Now locked in a position that means the cycle path is always available, the signal cabin that used to sit atop the central girder has been replaced by Pete Rogers' "Fisher of Dreams" sculpture. A poster on site explains why Rogers has the angler using the Flying Scotsman for bait and why the wiry dog is doing something unspeakable to the bike.

Should you wish you could continue along the path to walk or cycle back to the south-eastern outskirts of York, as the trail comes out at the former Challenor's Whin junction near to the Askham Bar park and ride.

But, going beyond the bridge, it is possible to scramble down the banking to the riverside. Walking carefully back towards the bridge, you can investigate some wonderfully massive and rusty cogs, wheels and other metallic structures that were part of the mechanism that allowed the bridge to swing.

*Venerable and rusty remnants in the swing mechanism chamber*

Once you've finished imagining the creaking and groaning that moving this mechanism required, return to the road, which bears the name 'York Road' throughout the village.

Re-cross the bridge, return to the pavement and walk back towards the village. To the right is York (formerly Naburn) Marina. Opened in 1970, this is one of the largest such facilities in the north of England with temporary and permanent moorings for up to 300 boats. Whilst freight traffic is now exceedingly rare this far up the Ouse, the number and variety of large pleasure craft moored here and along the riverbanks demonstrate the popularity of pleasure boating. The car park, cafe and shop are open to the general public. On the left are signs to Millbridge Farm. Naburn has had many mills over the years : Tour 4 has more detail on these mills.

Continuing towards the village you cross a tiny watercourse, Howden Dike, flowing on its way into the Ouse. For most of the year the Dike is a gentle stream draining the local fields, but you may spot a flood level measuring board. After heavy rainfall or rapid melting of snow in the Dales, the Ouse becomes swollen and waters from the Dike are not able to drain into the river, and 'back up' so covering the road. In extreme cases, this can make the roads impassable, and the levels indicated on the top of the marker are often reached.

Temporarily fork right off the B1222 to go along Front Street. On the left is the village Post Office, and, a very rare survival, a village Reading Room. A common sight a century or so ago, reading rooms making periodicals available for the working man to inform himself of the doings of the world are rare these days. Sadly, events of early 2022 seem to have caused both facilities to close. The bus shelter opposite has a good selection of local information. Further information is in the village phone box, converted into a mini Tourist Information Centre, a short walk away. The nearby street name, 'Ferry Farm Close' tells of the service formerly provided. At the end of Front Street is the private slipway for the former Ferry. This is now linked to the Yorkshire Ouse Sailing Club, founded 1938, whose clubhouse is based here.

There were once many ferries across the Ouse along its length but they have gradually been replaced by bridges, or ceased operating because of lack of demand. Naburn's fell into the latter category. Records from 1739 show a ferry just beyond Naburn Hall, but a few decades later a second ferry to Acaster Malbis on the far bank, accessed via a road past the Hall, provided competition. The extra road traffic irritated the Palmes family at Naburn Hall, so in 1824 they closed the road. The ferry service then moved to the modern position near the middle of the village.

In its final version, the ferry at Naburn was run on a chain system. A permanent chain fixed on the bed of the river rose up at slipways on each bank. A hand-cranked gear wheel fixed on the ferry engaged the chain and as the wheel was rotated, the vessel moved along the length of the chain and so across the river: a slow but simple method. The Ferry fell out of use in 1956.

Leaving the slipway on our right, to the left is Main Street, extending into the village from the slipway. On the left is the Blacksmith's Arms. Originally one of three such premises in the village, it was the 'Horse Shoe' by 1822, and gained its current title by 1872. A licensed premises has been on this site since 1750.

On the left at the junction with the B1222 is a typical village school. To continue the journey along the B1222, turn right here to go out of the village towards the village church. Although records of places of worship in Naburn go back many centuries, St. Matthew's was designed and built by that inveterate constructor of Victorian public buildings, G.T. Andrews. It opened in 1854 and is constructed of sandstone with a limestone spire and a Welsh slate roof. It is grade II listed. Modern access details are listed in the porch.

*Naburn Chain Ferry (courtesy naburnvillage.org)*

*The modern slipway : effectively an extension of 'Main Street'*

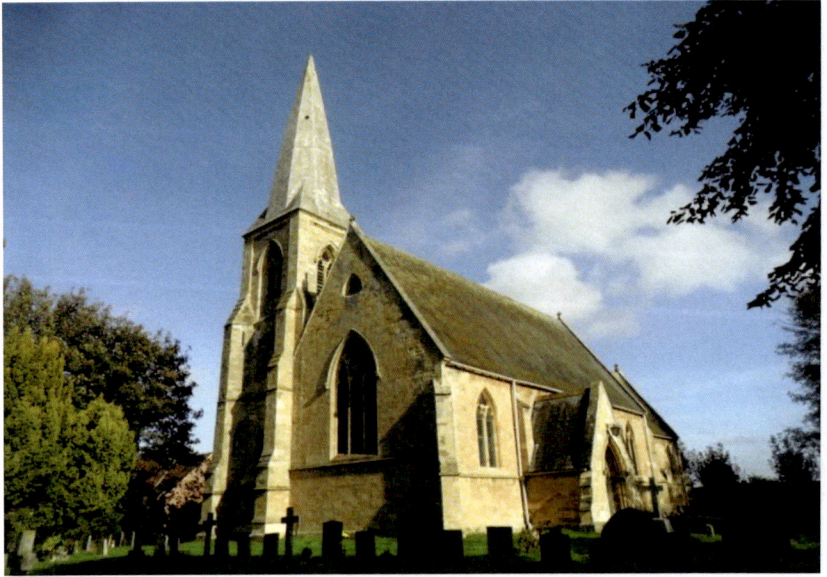

*St. Matthew's Church Naburn as seen in 2020 (above) and perhaps a century or so earlier (below) (courtesy of naburnvillage.org)*

Opposite the church is the entrance to the privately-owned Naburn Hall. First recorded as the Manor House of the Palmes family in 1345, it was rebuilt in 1735, greatly altered in 1818, further enlarged in 1870 and yet again in the early years of the 21st century. It is also grade II listed due to a proliferation of internal and external decorative features, as detailed by the site mentioned in the reference section. It is, however, very much a private residence today.

The excellent naburnvillage.org site has many more historic images and tales of village events and buildings.

Our journey now takes us a few hundred yards further along the B1222 to the Naburn Lock site.

*Naburn Ferry slipways on either bank in 2015 but a pleasure boat rather than a ferry is in shot - and the only customers in sight don't need any man-made assistance to make the crossing.*

## Transit 3 : Naburn Village to Naburn Locks

This is a very brief transit of a few hundred yards from Naburn village to the Naburn Lock complex. From the village, the road sweeps past Moor Lane, past the fingerpost pictured on page 20, as the river loops away to the right. You could combine the lock tour with the village one as there is a footpath along the grass verge next to the road. The junction to the lock complex is signposted to the right, at the site of two bus stops. Beyond a general shop on the right, a lane leads to the river. Although marked 'Private', access to the Lock is permitted. The river bus timetable is posted here. Follow the track to parking areas by the river. The river bus terminus is adjacent to the right. The walk from road to lock is about 400 yards.

## Tour 4 : Naburn Locks and Banqueting House

*View across Naburn Locks to the Banqueting House*

The Lock area displays the former importance of the Ouse in carrying trade to and from York, and the Banqueting Hall gives an idea of the wealth that could be obtained by controlling that trade.

A weir was constructed here, a mile or so downstream of Naburn in 1741, and the first lock was created in 1757. The developments of weir and lock helped ensure a navigable depth of water in the Ouse up to York, and to prevent the river being tidal there. It is claimed that these initial structures were the finest examples of contemporary waterway engineering in England.

Although the lock area is open to the public, it remains a working environment, so be prepared to follow instructions for your safety. The site is now controlled by the Canal and River Trust (C&RT) and there is a lock keeper on site.

The river management works created an island, which remains today, and a watermill which sadly does not. There have been many mills in Naburn, dating back to the 13th century. A windmill was recorded in 1345, which probably stood on Howden Dike near its confluence with the Ouse. In 1642 a Water-mill bridge was recorded in that locality.

Lingcroft mill, no doubt a windmill, was mentioned in 1354 and 1408. Lingcroft is at the north east end of the village. The name Mill Field is seen in 1476, adjacent to the river, north of Naburn. In 1697 a mill is recorded as standing near the Naburn to Water Fulford road, the forerunner of the B1222. The mill still existed in 1772.

By 1846-7 the only mill in the parish was that at Naburn Lock on the island between river and lock. Built between 1813 and 1817, it could only run when the tide meant the water level above the weir in the cut above the lock was significantly higher than that below the lock. Initially a corn mill, in the 1860s it was used to grind flint and stone for potteries in the West Riding, but then returned to grain. It was burnt down in 1877 but rebuilt. Damaged after another fire in 1913, on rebuilding, the wheel was replaced by a turbine. The mill ceased operation about 1955, and was demolished in 1958.

Returning to the locks, the current provision was built In two separate stages. As the dimensions of craft working to York increased, the original locks were too small, and a larger lock was built alongside. This was declared open by Queen Victoria's grandson, Prince Albert Victor, in 1888. The lock keepers' cottages adjacent to the lock, and the workshops and offices on the island were opened at the same time.

The C&RT sometimes opens these buildings to the public, where display boards tell the story and display contemporary images. The workshops contain a huge blacksmith's hearth, overhead pulleys, cogs, tools and shafts which give an indication of the kind of heavy engineering that could be carried out in relation to river craft and structures at Naburn.

The bridges that allow crossing of the locks have the five-lion badge of the City of York proudly displayed, making it clear under whose aegis the expansion of the site had occurred. The Ouse was a key trading highway to York in the 1880s, and the City fathers were keen to ensure that the trade flowed as easily (and profitably) as possible.

On the external wall of one of the buildings is a board marking the height of the river when in flood. From the many markings on it, it is clear that the lock site floods on a very regular basis. This is evidently damaging to 140-year old buildings, but it is not obvious what could reasonably and sympathetically be done to prevent this.

*An aerial view of the site, 1998. Banqueting Hall bottom right (courtesy of naburnvillage.org)*

A pleasant stroll can be had by walking some way upstream towards the Marina. In the opposite direction, you can walk a little way beyond the locks to observe the river glide around the corner. At this point, local youth used to come to bathe in the river and challenge each other to swim a 'width' of the river. **Given the proximity of the weir and the currents in the river this is <u>not</u> recommended.** Such activity might also annoy the anglers who are often at their bank-side perches.

Turning back towards the lock site, the fine Banqueting House was built in the Greek Revival style for the Trustees of the Ouse Navigation in 1823, The Trustees were mainly members of York Corporation. Their income derived from tolls on river craft and charges for mooring and loading and unloading. A report to the Corporation in the 1830s touched upon their failure as trustees to improve the state of the river, neglected for 30 years. Much was made of the contrast between this lethargy and the lavish spending of the trustees on the Banqueting Hall. The local press thundered that *'the trustees of the River Ouse certainly appear to have slumbered at their post and expenditure at Naburn Lock was the most indefensible part of their conduct'*.

Having lain forlornly empty for many years, the Hall has reopened as a cafe and arts and events venue. Although equally open to flooding threat, its future now looks more positive. It is a fine place to take tea on a sunny afternoon. Having been fortunate enough to attend a banquet in the premises in the 1970s, I can report that it was also a fine hall for drinking and dancing.

*Messrs. Acaster's Tug 'Little Shuva' and dumb barge 'River Star' approaching Naburn Locks from Cawood in the mid 1990s*

Traffic through the lock is now almost entirely restricted to private craft going to and from the Marina and York. The last regular freight flow was reels of newsprint destined for the then York Evening Press printing works in Walmgate, York. Massive rolls of paper were loaded on unpowered or 'dumb' barges and pushed upriver by tug to a specially-constructed wharf on the River Foss in Walmgate. This trade ceased in the 1990s.

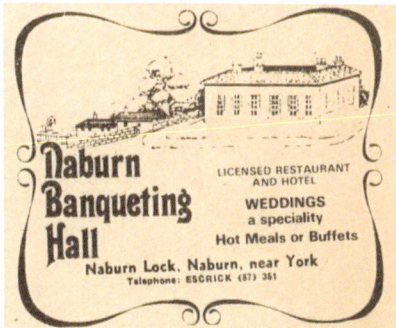

**Naburn Banqueting Hall**

LICENSED RESTAURANT AND HOTEL

WEDDINGS a speciality

Hot Meals or Buffets

Naburn Lock, Naburn, near York
Telephone: ESCRICK (87) 361

The lock area and island is also a fine venue for a relaxing stroll, some mild historic investigation and a picnic. Tables provided by C&RT await your wicker baskets and Thermos flasks, but access across the lock to the island may be restricted. Once replete, return to the top of the lane and turn right if you are in a car or on a bike, or cross the road to wait for the bus to continue to Stillingfleet To go back to York, turn left or use the bus stop adjacent to the junction for the Lock from the B1222.

*An advert showing the facilities of the Hall in 1980*

# Transit 4 : Naburn Locks to Stillingfleet

Somewhat of a longer journey now, from the City of York into North Yorkshire. The Ouse is our constant companion to the right: sometimes closer than others, but always there.

Passing the riding stables to the left, the road slopes down. At times of high water, the Ouse does flood the carriageway around here. In the following few hundred yards, the B1222 passes two historic, private houses.

On the left just before the road goes sharp left is the entrance to Bell Hall, a Grade I listed house, dated 1680, said to be built by John Etty for Sir John Hewley. Hewley had been MP for Pontefract 1658-60 and for York on three occasions around 1680. He founded what is now York Unitarian Chapel in St. Saviourgate. A supporter of the Protestant cause in the years before the Glorious Revolution of 1688/9, and of Parliament against the Crown, he famously objected to the rejection by King Charles II of the man elected to be Speaker of the House of Commons in these words

*"Shall we not have our tongue to speak our own words? ... The Speaker is our servant, and is he to obey his master, or not? Though the Speaker be the greatest commoner of England, yet he is not the greatest community of England. To have a servant imposed upon a man, though by the King himself, will not be suffered by any private master, or merchant; and shall the Commons of England endure it?"*

The architect John Etty was well known in the York area and was the father of the more widely recognised artist, William Etty. The house has many architectural flourishes both internally and externally. The website listed in the reference section records these. Now said to be a venue for weddings, perhaps you may be fortunate enough to be a guest and so be able to appreciate the finery.

As the road drops further towards the sharp left-hand bend, we pass over the tiny watercourse of Wood Dyke that marks the boundary between the City of York and the county of North Yorkshire, and in so doing enter the parish of Stillingfleet. Directly ahead is the second of our two notable halls, Moreby Hall.

This hall was built in 1828, and is grade II* listed. It is situated in extensive parkland leading down to the river, which used to be the site of the village of Moreby or Moorby, a name that aptly has Viking roots meaning 'farmstead on the marsh'.

The sharp double bend in the B1222 here is evidence of the influence of the landed gentry in former times. The original course of what became the road led straight on at the first bend, passing close by the house. Such proximity was taken exception to, so in 1829 the course of the road was diverted to the left away from Moreby Hall, and in 1844 a shorter section was further diverted around the edge of the park. The current course of the B1222 reflects these actions. Once around the second part of the double bend the original course of the road joins the current carriageway acutely from the right, with a post box at this entrance to the estate.

*Moreby Hall from the B1222*

The Moreby then Acclom families had the estate from the 14th century, on payment of a unique rent : a red rose delivered to the Sherriff of York. Monuments to both families can be seen in St. Helen's at Stillingfleet. A later family, the Prestons, endowed the current village hall there, with a plaque over the door recording this donation in 1927.

The double bend marks the entry of the B1222 into the parish of Stillingfleet, and the road's next royal connection, the 'boar badge'. The boar was the symbol of King Richard III, and metal detectorists working in 2010 in "fields near Stillingfleet" found one of the 13000 silver gilt badges Richard had had made for his son's investiture at York Minster in 1483. After losing to Henry Tudor at Bosworth two years later, Ricardians weren't so keen to be associated with the losing team : the theory is the badge was thrown away. The boar is now penned at the Yorkshire Museum in York where the dirt of 500 years has been removed to reveal a glint of gold, two remaining legs and "impressive genitalia".

A few fields further on, to the right, is the venue of another sad loss. A tree-ringed field is the former ground of Stillingfleet CC : founded in 1934, but the twin perils of abysmal weather and alternative Saturday afternoon attractions apparently caused the club to have to abandon regular home games a few years ago for financial reasons. The forlorn pavilion looks on as agricultural enclosures engulf the outfield. The B1222 now approaches Stillingfleet. To the left is an unusual sight in the Vale of York : elevated ground. This so-called Escrick moraine joins the B1222 at the far side of the village, and it will be described in part of Tour 5 that follows.

# Tour 5 : Stillingfleet

*The essence of the village scene. The village bus, operated by a village company (Jaronda of Cawood) on a service connecting villages to major towns picks up passengers opposite a notable village church. Sadly neither bus nor operator from this 1990s view survive, but the No. 42 still serves the villages.*

The name Stillingfleet derives from the Old English 'Styfelingafleot'. 'the stretch of river ("le flet" as it was known in the 13th century) belonging to Styfel and his followers'. The village is mentioned in the Domesday book as Steflingefled

The historic highlight of the village is the grade1 listed St. Helen's church, but there are other pleasantries to take in first. There is parking space on The Green, a right turn off the B1222 just before the bridge. Assuming you have parked there, a possible tour is as follows.

Walk towards the bridge and use it to cross the beck. The B1222 is now carried over it on a fine stone bridge of 1820. The beck seems placid as it runs its course to drain into the Ouse: a plaque on the bridge tells of the terrible floods of March 1947 when its depth reached 21 feet. Further plaques describe the provision of the lanterns in 1902 to mark the coronation of King Edward VII, and their renewal in 1992.

The B1222 now becomes 'Church Hill' and on the right is the Methodist Chapel of 1819. At the top of the hill is a fine village pub, the Cross Keys, serving since at least1889, but currently closed. The slope you have ascended has taken you to the crest of the Escrick moraine at the T junction This is the ridge mentioned in the previous transit. It has quite a geologic and historic importance.

Beloved of GCSE Geography teachers, a terminal moraine marks the furthest extent of the advance of a glacier. All the solid material a glacier has scraped from the underlying ground is pushed to its front edge. As the ice melts and the glacier retreats, this material is dumped and left behind, forming what passes for a hill in the notoriously flat Vale of York. Viking invaders may well have trudged back along this ridge to their boats moored at nearby Kelfield

Back at the bottom of the slope you can walk across the Green to look at the bridge and its warning depth board, or stroll past pleasant properties.

Cross the bridge and bear left to a plant nursery, and a tea rooms or continue along past the Village Institute of 1927, with its Jubilee Gates of 1977 and the cemetery, containing a fine cross of remembrance.

*Pub sign, village memorial and bestial carving at St. Helen's church*

But it is now time to turn our attention to St. Helen's. This is best approached by walking back to the lych gate and then up to the south-west face of the church. The church dates from the mid 12th century. It is a most tranquil setting today, but the foundation of the church in 1154 AD came as the 19 years of civil war and "anarchy" between King Stephen and Queen Matilda raged in England was ending. Tranquilly must have been even more prized then.

The tower and clock that face you are certainly admirable, but the south west doorway and its carvings are the initial highlight here.

Fantastic (in both senses of the word) carvings around the South West door depict all manner of mythical beasts, and exaggerated human faces, along with typical Norman designs such as chevrons and "beakheads". The variety and quality of the carving is breathtaking : this is one of the finest pieces of 12th century sculpture in England. An adjacent notice gives more detail.

The meaning behind the carving is unclear. Perhaps the grotesque figures represent the evils of this world we have to pass before reaching the sanctuary of the church. The regal image atop the arch is presumed to be of King Henry II, the monarch in 1154, the year the church was founded.

*St.Helen's Church, SW doorway, with the noble image of King Henry II at the keystone of the arch.*

Fabulous though all this carving is, the real highlight of St. Helen's lies inside. The South West door is not usually open, but around the corner, to the north, a smaller door allows access.

Whilst both doors currently fitted in these fine arches are of high quality, the one you are about to enter through is but a copy of the 'real thing'.

Inside the church, hanging on the wall, preserved after eight centuries of battling the Yorkshire weather is a door like no other. Research by many hands, most tellingly by Messrs Addyman and Goodall in 1975 and published in *Archaeoligica Vol CVI* in 1979, (see reference section) this door dates to at least the foundation of the church and perhaps two centuries earlier.

Having served for many centuries, it was 'brought inside' in 1990.

*The 'Viking Door' inside St. Helen's, Stillingfleet*

The door is divided into two by horizontal strips of metal twined together with elaborate skill. There are two hinges, both in the shape of huge letter C's : letters that end in dragon's heads. In the upper left section are two figures thought to represent Adam and Eve. Adam is reaching for an apple from a now-vanished tree in the region that now has a circle of nails. Below is an unusual, convoluted cross that has been said to be the cross of the 5th century St. Brigid of Kildare, a form of Christian good luck charm, to be hung in windows and over doorways.

Another dragon's head can be seen on the prow of the image of a Viking longship. This may be a reference to the Viking presence at the Battle of Fulford in 1066. If the door had been made in the mid 12th century, that event would still be strong in the folk memory. Some say that the Viking ship dates back to earlier times when Viking raiding parties would regularly sail the Ouse, but evidence for a 10th century origin is inconclusive. All in all, an amazing piece of work, an amazing survival of at least 800 years. Extensive information about the door is given inside the church.

Before leaving the church, take time to look at the effigy of Sir Robert de Moreby in the side chapel. Lord of the Manor of Stillingfleet, he fought alongside King Edward III in campaigns in Scotland between 1310 and 1320.

*The tomb of Sir Robert de Moreby*

Regularly open during daytimes, St. Helen's, with its unique and evocative door and exquisite stone archways, is certainly a place for any fan of history to inspect.

Amazingly, however, there is yet another item of great interest at the site. This is to be found in the burial ground between the church and the road. Somewhat obscured and displaced by conifer trees is the memorial to those who died in the "Stillingfleet Tragedy" of Boxing Day 1833. A little beyond the memorial, and towards the road is the final resting place of one of the survivors, Richard Toes. The full story of this calamity that claimed the lives of 11 villagers is told in the next transit. on page 61 and 62.

*Memorial to a tragedy and the lych gate*

Once you have taken in all the wonders of St. Helen's, walk to the lych gate and return to your car. 'Lych' derives from the Saxon word for a corpse. The gate was the place where a coffin and bearers could shelter before a funeral.. It also marks the demarcation between consecrated and unconsecrated ground.

To continue the journey, drive up Church Hill, turn right at the junction where the B1222 meets the Ice Age moraine, to leave Stillingfleet en route to Cawood.

If you take the bus from the bay by the lych gate it will take you to Cawood via the back roads through the hamlet of Kelfield, part of the Stillingfleet parish. The bus to return to York can be boarded at the stop between the former village Post Office and the Village Institute.

# Transit 5 : Stillingfleet to Cawood

In a few hundred yards, we leave behind the final houses of Stillingfleet to return to open countryside. For the next mile and a half or so the road gradually drops away as we effectively enter the true flood plain of the Ouse. Whilst at times of high water, the river does submerge the road on both sides of Naburn, unless the river is very high, the surrounding fields are not inundated. As the road is now dropping down to cross the Ouse at Cawood, the plain that does become inundated becomes apparent. This stretch of the river was also the site of a terrible yuletide accident, the "Stillingfleet Tragedy". This unfolded on the reach of the river across the fields to our right, where the site of Stillingfleet Landing lies at the end of a track on the far side of the hedge as the road veers left at what is known locally as 'Gypsy Corner'.

On Boxing Day 1833, fourteen church singers from Stillingfleet, as had become traditional, set out to sing Christmas songs around various parish locations. The itinerary included Moreby, Stillingfleet and Kelfield, all on this side of the river, but also Acaster Selby, on the far bank.

A boat was therefore needed. As it was Boxing Day, the party decided to give the ferryman who operated a service across to Acaster Selby a festive day off. Instead, they used a vessel owned by one of the singers, John Turner, who was used to the river. Unfortunately, it was rowed by two men, John Fisher and George Eccles, who were not. Tragedy struck around 4:30, towards the end of the day, in gathering gloom and bitter cold. The trip should have been an easy and joyful one. The tide was with the boat as it travelled towards their disembarkment point at Stillingfleet Landing. The Acaster call was the last one of the day, and all aboard could look forward to a Boxing Day evening at home in front of a warming fire.

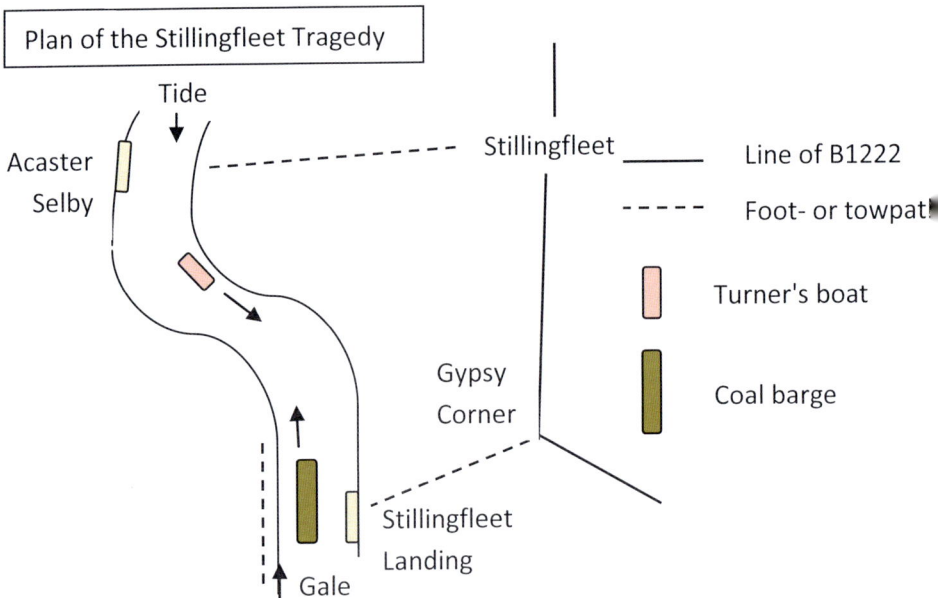

Plan of the Stillingfleet Tragedy

The landing was round a bend in the river. As the boat turned that bend, they saw a fully-laden sail-powered coal barge heading towards them. Whilst the tide was against it, there was a strong wind in its favour, bearing with it rain and snow. It was also being pulled by rope attached to a horse on the Acaster bank tow path. This vision was no doubt a shock, but there was plenty of space on the Stillingfleet side to pass the barge safely by.

But Turner suddenly ordered that the boat make for the Acaster bank. Fisher and Eccles bowed to experience and obeyed. It can only be presumed that Turner believed the tow rope would sag into the river, and his craft and the 14 souls aboard could safely pass over it.

There seems to have been confusion as to whether Turner shouted to the horseman to 'tighten' or 'lighten' the tow rope. Whichever action was taken, the current did not allow the rope to sink and, in attempting to hoist the rope over the craft, it snagged on the stern. The unyielding momentum of the barge capsized the boat. Two men were rescued at once by the barge, a third survived by clinging onto the oars, but despite cries for help from the eleven others in the river, the current swept them, in their sodden, woollen clothes, to their deaths. Over the course of the next few days, nine of the bodies were recovered from the river and are interred at St Helen's, Stillingfleet.

At the inquest it was pondered why Turner had chosen to go between the barge and Acaster bank, when there was sufficient space on the Stillingfleet side. No one could offer a reason for this, and as Turner was one of the dead, he was not able to explain his decision. The inquest delivered a verdict that all had 'accidentally drowned'.

*The memorials to the victims of the Stillingfleet tragedy, at St. Helen's Church, Stillingfleet.*

As the B1222 curves left to Cawood, in a field entrance on the right, a gate guards the track to a pumping station, installed in the late 20th century to help prevent flooding. To the left of this, a hedge-bordered track marks the boundary of Stillingfleet parish, leading towards the site of the Landing, A gate prevents access to the riverbank, but there is little to see at the site today. Stillingfleet Landing was marked on OS maps until the 1950s, but had disappeared by the time the 1969 'Six inch' series was published. No trace now remains of the staithe.

The twists and turns that make this stretch of the B1222 so attractive to bikers, as described in the section on Squires Café (page 103/4), reveal themselves over the next mile or so.

These curves come to an end at the fork to the left to the hamlet of Kelfield, as the B1222 bends to the right. Ahead lies a ¾-mile long straight, commonly known as Ferry Lane, that leads the B1222 into Cawood. Created in 1814, for ready access across marshy land to Cawood Ferry, nowadays for obvious reasons it is a place where throttles are often fully opened: for equally obvious reasons, a place where police cars often observe proceedings !

This flood plain of the Ouse is Kelfield Ings, designed to be submerged to protect Cawood and the habitations to Selby and beyond. The word "ings" again shows Viking influence, being a old Norse word for a water meadow or marsh, particularly as part of a flood plain. When the river does overtop the impressive earthworks of the banking, the effects are dramatic. To give an idea of how dramatic, when the river floods, the hedge to the left of Ferry Lane is entirely under water.

This inundation does bring fertility to the soil, but it also ruins the crop planted there at the time. There have been at least five inundations this century. Even after the river levels subside it can take at least a fortnight for the B1222 to be free of mud and water to be passable again and longer again for the fields to be workable.

At the end of Ferry Lane, the road takes a left hand turn as a three storey house oversees proceedings. This is the former Ferryboat Inn (and my former home!) of 1821, and in the days when there was a Ferry at Cawood, the house lay to the left of the road. Ferry travellers continued up what is now the private track to the house and caught the ferry from in front of that dwelling. All that changed when the swing bridge was ready for use in 1871. The road was moved so that the Inn was to its right, and the Inn, having lost its purpose of welcoming and giving sustenance to travellers before the crossing was made, went out of business in 1872.

Although the river often looks placid, currents can run strongly and there are records of accidents and drownings. One passage that is fabled rather than actually recorded was that of highwayman Dick Turpin who is alleged to have crossed here as part of his infamous London to York ride, as described in William Ainsworth's novel 'Rookwood'. To Ainsworth, Turpin was a romantic hero. Chased by his pursuers, Turpin reached the Sherburn bank at daybreak to find the ferryman resting on the York side. The ferryman was hailed, but before he can scull across, the pack is at Turpin's heels. Summoning Black Bess to a final effort, hero and steed brave the water, swim to safety and gallop away up Ferry Lane. Inspect the river here to judge quite how fanciful this scenario is.

The iron swing-bridge was a toll bridge until taken over by the County in 1882. The cabin gives the bridgemaster a fine view along the river for approaching vessels that normally radio ahead for "permission for a swing". Extended to its current size around 1980, until the 1990s such was the level of commercial river traffic, the cabin was permanently manned. But as trade declined, there is a presence for merely two hours either side of high tide, in daylight hours. A mooring platform downstream of the bridge is provided for tall craft arriving outside hours when the cabin is manned.

Despite being 70 miles from the sea, the Ouse remains tidal at Cawood. When the moon's gravity has an exceptional effect, a minor "bore" or river wave passes through Cawood at turn of the tide. This locally has the Norse name "aegir". As for road traffic, although recently strengthened to allow vehicles weighing up to 10 tonnes to cross, feats of reversing are regularly undertaken by drivers of vehicles somewhat larger than that. Ill-programmed satnavs or unaccountable invisibility of warning signs are clearly at fault !

The bridge swings gracefully open in a horizontal plane. In high summer, parts of the bridge have been known to expand so that the bridge cannot reclose safely, leading to extensive traffic delays and detours via Selby or Tadcaster. Until 1974, this crossing was from the East Riding of Yorkshire to the West. Old counties or new, the transit from Stillingfleet is now complete. To tour Cawood, venture across and park up on Old Road (see map, page 70). Bus travellers alight at the village Post Office.

*Traction Engine Anne checks the weight limit on the bridge (above). In 2020 the former Ferry Boat Inn looks down on the original course of the road to the right, and the post -1872 diversion to the left.*

C A W O O D   C A S T L E.

Records talk of a horse ferry, seemingly operating in the foreground, although not with 'Bess' on board on this occasion. The gate in a brick housing presumably holds back the Bishopdyke - of which more in the next few pages.  Below, the "Ferry Boat Inn" on the York bank, pictured in 1870, just before the bridge was built.

# Tour 6 : Cawood

The modern pronunciation of 'Cawood' is as if it was a name, 'K. Wood'. Older inhabitants and the historical record suggest that it was once spoken as "Caw -wood" in imitation of the call of crows in the adjacent woodland. The village remains wooded in places and there are plenty of members of the corvid family in residence. Others suggest that 'Ca' indicates a hollow by a wood, producing a sound of "Ca-ood". However you say it, Cawood is one of the oldest settlements in the Selby district, lying on the west bank of the Ouse, just downstream of its confluence with the Wharfe.

*All Saints' Church, Cawood*

The earliest historical record of Cawood comes in 937 AD when King Athelstan granted the castle to Archbishop Wulfstan. By 963 King Edgar granted the Sherburn estate, which included Cawood, to the Archbishop of York. But this grant was more to do with the area around Sherburn rather than Cawood, as part of the village owned by the de Cawood family was not included. Their moated manor at Keesbury was kept separate : this site is mentioned in the tour of Cawood that follows.

As a result of this division, Cawood has had an unusual pattern of growth, in three areas. One around Keesbury, another around the river crossing and a third around the church, which, as was common, was placed on the highest piece of land in the village.

In his well-known popular history series, Arthur Mee dubbed Cawood the 'Windsor of the North', to mark the several royal visits to the Castle. It is probable that the Saxon king, Athelstan, had the first fortification built at Cawood, on the current site, in the tenth century. The stone came to Cawood via the Bishopdyke (see the next transit) from quarries near Sherburn. By the twelfth century, Cawood had become a residence for the Archbishops of York, mentioned in the historical records in 1181 before being converted into a "quadrangular castle", one based on a rectangular floor plan, during 1374 and 1388.

Kings John and Henry III passed through briefly, Edward I kept his court here for seven years whilst he tried to 'hammer' the Scots, Edward II licked his wounds in Cawood after defeat at Bannockburn and Henry VIII came calling with wife no.5, Catherine Howard in 1541.

George Neville became Archbishop of York in 1465. The Archbishop's brother, Earl of Warwick, planned a celebratory feast a year later. In an example of medieval one-upmanship, common in the times of the Wars of the Roses, he planned the feast to be more extensive than that of King Edward IV, five years earlier.

Guests included the Duke of Gloucester, the King's brother. Dubbed the 'Great Feast of Cawood' it lasted several days, and records show the gargantuan quantity of food consumed. Over 200 aspiring medieval Masterchef contestants had at least 104 oxen, 6 wild bulls, 400 swans, 1000 capons and 104 peacocks to deal with. Around 25,000 gallons of wine helped wash it all down. A plaque in the 'Ferry Inn' lists the full menu.

All that remains of the Cawood Castle structures today are the Banqueting Hall and the Gatehouse, both mentioned on the Cawood tour that follows. Some say that Cawood Castle is the source of the rhyme 'Humpty Dumpty' referring to the political fall of Cardinal Wolsey whilst here in 1530.

The village saw a skirmish in the Civil War, and at the end of hostilities, the Castle, having briefly served as a prisoner of war camp, was destroyed as a military outpost.

In the 18th century, Cawood was described as a market town, and crossing point of the Ouse on the way to or from York. It was sufficiently important to have a rail line built from Selby, opened in 1898. The line was partly intended as a cut across from the Leeds-Selby line to Church Fenton on the Leeds-York line, but never made it past Cawood. Passenger services survived until 1929 and a largely agricultural goods service until 1960. Whilst the course of the line is visible on maps, no tangible relics remain for public inspection. Hartley's history of the line is detailed in the reference section.

The tour described on the following pages takes you around the historical heart of Cawood.

Should you wish a more extensive tour, look up North Yorkshire's free "Wolsey Walk" that takes in other parts of the village, and if you are of an investigative bent, a treasure trail leaflet can be purchased on line (see reference section). To follow the map below, walk back towards the bridge and start from the area known as 'Bridge Foot'.

As you look towards the village, on the right is the timbered 'Bridgekeeper's Cottage'. A small plaque on the wall records the water level on the last occasion the village flooded, in 1982. On that side of the road, King Street takes you to the Ferry Inn (formerly 'The Commercial').

Today Cawood has three pubs - which is certainly sufficient, but in living memory, there were many more. Eschewing the temptations of the 'Ferry' continue on to pass in front of one of these others, the 'Thompsons Arms' that served its last in 1994. Across the lights is Market Place which, as described on page 71, was home to more.

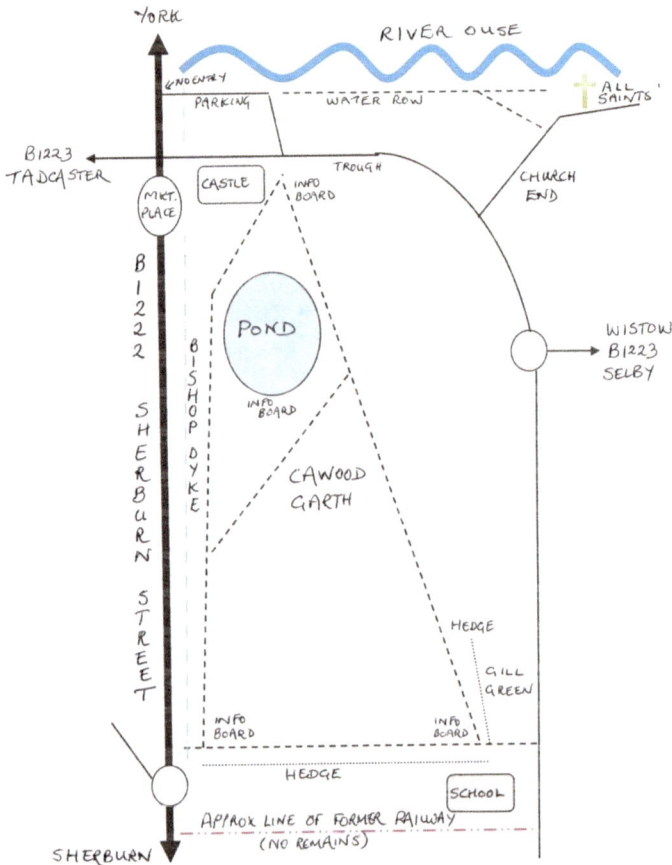

SKETCH MAP for CAWOOD WALK
NOT TO SCALE : NOT ALL ROADS SHOWN

*The 'Tour de Yorkshire' visits Cawood with the former Ferryboat Inn looking on*

Cawood's Market Day was Wednesday, but the last stall holders packed up around 200 years ago. Market trading is thirsty work : in the 20th century, Cawood had 13 licensed premises. One of these former hostelries, the Anchor Inn, now hosts a different form of spiritual succour, as the base for a Gurdjieff retreat. Next door, yet another that's called its last 'Last Orders', the Burleigh House Hotel. Happily, across the road, the Jolly Sailor still plies its trade.

Facing you is the Mill House. The style of the property frontages in this part of the village display their former commercial identity, so, along with the existence of a Market Place, that justifies the old description of Cawood as a town, but such commerce has declined since the 1960s. The road narrows to become Sherburn Street. On the right-hand side is the former Methodist Chapel, now flats, and almost opposite, the former Gas Works.

As you approach the mini roundabout the Parish Pump - formerly a source of both village water and village gossip - nestles in the trees. A simple wooden bridge takes you over a watercourse. This is the Bishopdyke, which accompanies the B1222 to Sherburn. More of its story later. Just before the mini roundabout, to the left was Cawood Station, the terminus of a five-mile long rural branch into Selby. Sylvan Close now occupies the site. New houses on the right of the mini roundabout mark the former 'Bay Horse' : another lost hostelry.

Return to the wooden bridge to access Cawood Garth; a fabulous open area based on the medieval enclosure of the Castle, saved for the village in the 1980s by determined villagers and the presence of Great Crested Newts. The Garth is a Scheduled Ancient Monument.

You now have two choices: follow the tarmac path by the hedge to come out at Gill Green, or cut across the Garth, past the pond to come out next to the Castle.

Let's follow the hedge to the gate onto Broad Lane. The line of the railway was approximately that of the hedge on the far side of the school field. Coming out on Broad Lane, rail fans could walk past the school to see a strip of grass beyond 'Gatekeeper's Cottage' and conclude this is where the track crossed the road. Otherwise, turn left towards the horse chestnut trees, planted on Gill Green in 1937. Apparently destined to be the village's way of marking the coronation of Edward VIII, but he abdicated before they could be planted so they were dedicated to George VI instead. As you proceed towards the mini roundabout, on the right is the site of Keesbury Manor - one of the three 'centres' of Cawood referred to earlier, and a site of regular archaeological digs. Go left at the mini roundabout. Another house name reminds us of the village's past : the 'blue lamp' shone outside the old Police House until the 1970s.

*The pond on Cawood Garth - the former grounds of the Castle*

Another diversion is possible at the junction. Either bear left at the white railings or be seduced by the fabulous gable ends of Yew Tree House on the corner and proceed right, along Church End to All Saints' Church, parts of which date back to the 12th century, and is normally open during daylight hours. All Saints' is not quite in St. Helen's' league perhaps, but is the epitome of a village church, with fine stained glass and a fascinating memorial to Cawood-born Archbishop Mountain. On the river-facing exterior what is said to be a medieval tomb cover faintly displays a stem and four circles in the wall between two windows. Venturing further along Church End allows you to view more fine gable ends and a row of Victorian almshouses.

Return along a path with the flood wall at your immediate right and pass a pumping station. This is Water Row. For most of the year the Ouse is far away in its channel : but water levels approaching the coping stones of the wall are not unknown in winter.

Bear left up Old Road to meet Thorpe Lane, At the top, immediately to your left is the former Old Girls' School, in front of which are two 'super' petrol pumps that have long since ceased to be in 'regular' service. Meet up again with tourists who have visited neither Gill Green nor the church across the road by an old cattle drinking trough outside the village's former wood yard.

Continue towards the traffic lights, passing Cawood Castle Gatehouse and Banqueting Hall on your left. These buildings are Grade I listed and currently owned by the Landmark Trust. They are available for holiday visits, but not open to casual public inspection.

*Cawood Castle Gatehouse and Banqueting Hall*

It was from here in 1530 that Cardinal Wolsey, beloved of the villagers, was summoned to London in disgrace by Henry VIII following his failure to sort out Henry's divorce from Katharine of Aragon. Perhaps thankfully for the cardinal, he died on the journey south at Leicester, where he is buried.

# Cawood Castle

All that remains of Cawood Castle is the stone-built 15th century Gatehouse with the largely brick-built Banqueting Hall to its side. The Castle was the principal palace of the Archbishops of York from the 13th century until 1646 when Parliament ordered it 'slighted', or made untenable, and decrenellated, after the Civil War.

*Castle Gatehouse, 1899*

The Castle has had many royal visitors over the years, with Kings John, Henry III, Edward I, wife Margaret, Edward II and wife Isabella and Henry VIII accompanied by wife number five, Catherine Howard, all eligible to sign the visitors' book. The final two couples didn't have happy times after leaving Cawood. Edward met his Waterloo at Bannockburn whilst Catherine later met the sharp edge of an axe after dalliances with Thomas Culpeper, another castle guest.

The Gatehouse was built from stone sourced at Huddlestone, a little further along the modern B1222, in the time of Archbishop John Kempe. Described by Henry VI as *one of the wisest lords in the land*' he gained the mitre in York in 1425. In 1439 he became a Cardinal, and it is surely not by chance that several finely-carved stone Cardinal-style hats and wheatsheaves that appear in Kempe's coat of arms decorate the Gatehouse's archway. Such sheaves were the symbol of another Kempe, whose stained glass is on view at All Saints'.

During the Civil War, the castle changed hands three times. Originally held by Royalist forces, they deserted in October 1642 when 600 or so Parliamentarians approached. However, the king's men were in charge again by June of the next summer only for the military under Sir John Meldon to recapture it for Cromwell's side in 1644.

The  building continued to be used by the York Archbishops as a 'Court Leet' : in simple terms one responsible for local matters and small-scale infractions. Such courts were common throughout the land, and officers of Courts Leet included such as *chimney peepers* (to make sure your chimney was swept),  *scavengers* (to make sure the lanes and privies were hygienic) and the *pinherd* (to make sure stray livestock were kept in the village Pinfold. Cawood has a Pinfold Cottage on Water Row). Such courts were finally abolished by Parliament in 1977, but Cawood's had long ceased prior to that. In 1932, the courtroom was turned into a sitting room, and then, in WW2,  an Officers' Mess.

The Landmark Trust acquired the building in 1985, and, following sympathetic and extensive renovation, reinstatement of some crenellation and erection of a metallic wheat sheaf on the roof to honour Kempe, it is now a holiday let.

*Stone sheaves and mitres at the Gatehouse*

*B1222/B1223 crossroads in Cawood with inaccurate caption (1930s) (oldbarnsley.com)*

To complete the walk, return to the lights and turn right to go down High Street, past the former Thompsons Arms to the Car Park. The large brick building ahead controls water flow between river and Bishopdyke. The brazier on the telegraph pole to the right was part of the chain of beacons for Queen Elizabeth's Golden Jubilee. Since then it has become the site for village firework displays.

Taking great care with traffic, you can venture onto the bridge to inspect a plaque marking the bridge's completion. The heavy-duty breakwaters are needed to prevent ill-prepared skippers falling foul of treacherous currents that bridge supports engender in a river. Depth boards indicate how swollen the river can become. In extreme flooding, the river wets the bridge's deck.

*Procession at Church End, November 1930. The 400th anniversary of Wolsey's removal from Cawood*

# Transit 6 : Cawood to Bishopwood

Having taken time to experience much of what Cawood offers, it is now the moment to resume the journey along the B1222. Return to the traffic lights and head directly away from the bridge. Unfortunately, the No 42 bus can no longer help you and there is virtually no public transport provision between here and Sherburn.

*Sherburn Street to the left , the Garth to the right and the Bishopdyke*

The B1222 passes through Market Place and becomes Sherburn Street as it heads towards the mini roundabout at the edge of the village: a clear clue to where we are headed! But almost at once it becomes Bishopdyke Road. Although these days it seems little more than a large field drain, the Bishopdyke has a long and noble history, and the B1222 bears that name on older maps all the way between Cawood and the outskirts of Sherburn.

Rising from a spring close to Huddlestone Quarries (see page 104) the Bishopdyke is a six mile-long man-made waterway that runs from the quarry site to the spot adjacent to the bridge at Cawood where it enters the Ouse. It is culverted for the final 50 yards or so of that journey, but as the B1222 makes its way to Sherburn, the Bishopdyke accompanies the road closely.

The waterway was used to transport limestone from the quarries onto the Ouse and thence further afield. Stone came this way not only to build Cawood Castle, but also York Minster, Eton College and Kings' College Cambridge. Small loads of grain and agricultural material were also carried. A YTV programme from the 1980s (if memory serves) once followed this journey. The recent flood-control gates on the dyke to the left prevent such a trip today.

As you leave Cawood, the Bishopdyke is channelled across and beneath the road at Tile Bridge. Formerly a fruit farm on a tight double bend, now dwellings in extensive grounds on a gentle curve. Just beyond the village on the right, set back a little from the road are the private grounds of what is now Stockbridge Technology Centre (STC). This was set up as a government research station in 1948 with the aim of increasing home-grown food production. The famous rhubarb triangle is only a few miles away from Stockbridge as the crow flies and with favourable soil, extensive glasshouses and a trained staff, research into improving rhubarb to enable it to compete against imported fruit was one of many projects undertaken.

Varieties such as Stockbridge Arrow, Stockbridge Guardsman and Cawood Delight were successfully introduced. Support for such agricultural research waned over the years, however and the centre was only saved from closure in 2001 by the efforts of commercial growers. It became a limited company and charitable trust aimed at agricultural innovation, experimentation and education. Rhubarb research is largely in the past, but the centre's name proudly lives on in the tasty cultivars it developed.

*Entrance to the private grounds at Stockbridge*

For the next mile or so, as we travel over Cawood Common, the Dyke parallels the road to its right, with several simple bridges allowing access to fields. However, a sharp bend to the left marks the start of another deviation. The original course of the road is now merely a private farm track passing under the East Coast Main Line (ECML) to the right. If you are following things on older maps, at this point, the line of the B1222 marked a parish boundary. The line of that boundary shows the original line of the road.

The new B1222 is carried in a curve over the ECML. To the left the woods of Bishopwood can be seen, the venue for the next tour. The car park to the left is usually closed to the public, so to make sure you can find somewhere to park, continue with the road over the bridge and turn left at the crossroads along Scalm Lane. Just before you do this, the old course of the road re-joins the new at a sharp angle on the right.

*The old (left) and new courses of the B1222: Sherburn side of the ECML bridge*

The RAF closed its Church Fenton base in 2013 and it is now a civil airport, 'Leeds East'. It also houses former hangars used as sound stages for TV productions such as in the recent 'Victoria' TV series, first aired in 2016. .

As the sign suggests, Scalm Park has a golf course and contains an intriguing World War 2 survivor : a dummy control tower meant to act as a night-time decoy to distract enemy planes intent on attacking the fighter squadrons based at Church Fenton. This is not available for public inspection, but the website in the reference section gives the full story

*Road sign at the junction of the B1222 with Scalm Lane, c. 2005. Oh for the days when a 'phone box rated a mention on a road sign!*

77

# Tour 7 : Bishopwood

Once on Scalm Lane, follow the road to recross the railway. The woods seen from the B1222 are now on both sides. Continue along Scalm Lane for a half mile or so to a car park on the left. Bishop Wood, is an area of about 850 acres of mixed woodland managed by the Forestry Commission. The majority of the mature timber currently standing is around a century old as the older trees were felled to meet the needs for timber for World War 1. However, a forested area has been on this site for many more years than that.

The name derives from it being at one stage in the ownership of the Archbishop of York, and the fact that it falls inside the episcopal 'Liberty of Cawood, Wistow and Otley' confirms that thought. The path of the B1222 as we journeyed from Cawood marked that legal boundary.

The 'Liberty' was an area of 13 townships and associated land under the rulings of a court and was a separate criminal jurisdiction run by magistrates under the jurisdiction of the Archbishop. This Liberty had been given by King Athelstan to the Archbishop. Earliest surviving written records date from 1789. It was, however, not very busy: in its final ten years, only 51 cases were brought before the bench until its absorption into the West Riding court system in 1864.

Having safely parked up, there are many tracks that encourage you to take a stroll - but a stroll that can often be muddy. Recent work has felled some of the trees to allow light to flood into glades, encouraging the growth of woodland flowers. Some of this felled wood has been left to stand and decay to provide habitats for invertebrates and fungi, further encouraging the birds and small mammals that feed on them. This scrubby appearance is a deliberate policy to increase biodiversity.

The fact that your stroll might be muddy isn't part of these recent developments. Study of old Ordnance Survey maps shows features with names that hint at the damp nature of the wood.

For instance, 'West Hagg Plain', lying to the south-east has a name that means a 'firm place in a bog' and one of the paths in the northerly section of the wood is called 'Hammer Sike', a sike being a stream that runs through a marshy area. 'Dam Head Road' has implications that needs no updating.

There are records of the wood being used as a royal hunting area. When King John stayed at Cawood Castle in the early 13th. century, records show that he hunted in the wood. Another track bearing the name 'Royal Oak Road' indicates the route along which he might have travelled, and there are various 'Closes' where a royal party could have taken their ease in a sunlit glade. These names now only exist on the largest-scale maps and are unmarked on the ground.

Activity in the wood could be deadly for humans as well as wildlife. The Rev. Sabine Baring Gould, composer of 'Onward Christian Soldiers', refers in his book 'Yorkshire Oddities, Incidents and Strange Events' to a 17th. century incident, as follows.

*"On the Monday following Palm Sunday, the 14th of April, 1690, William Barwick, a man living in Cawood, took his wife a stroll along a pleasant lane leading to Bishop Wood, then an extensive tract of forest trees, and even now one of the wildest and most picturesque spots in the neighbourhood of Selby.*

*Mary Barwick was expecting her confinement at no great distance of time. William made her walk before him; they crossed the little bridge over Bishop's Dyke, and entered a close or field where was a pond. It was surrounded by thick rushes, and the willows were covered with their silken tufts, unrifled by the children for "palms" on the preceding day.*

*William Barwick looked round. No one was in sight. He seized his wife, threw her into the pond, and did not let go his hold till she was drowned. When he was quite satisfied that life was extinct, he drew the body out of the water, and concealed it among the rushes. He then returned home."*

Barwick was eventually arrested, then tried and convicted at York on September 18th., 1690, and subsequently executed. No reason was ever ascertained for the felony.

Occasionally a rushing noise will be heard disturbing the peace of the woodland setting. This will be a train passing on the adjacent ECML, which sliced a small area off the wood during its construction, to ensure that the curve in the line as it headed north was sufficiently gentle to not hinder high-speed running.

If you've taken so much exercise that you feel peckish, refreshments might be available at Scalm Park Leisure Village, which as part of a golf course and chalet resort does offer food - but please check ahead. If that's your destination, turn left onto Scalm Lane, and it is on the right at the bend at the end of the straight..

If you're ready to explore further, it's time to return to the B1222. Turn right onto Scalm Lane and follow the road back over the tracks and to the junction. But before going any further along the road, time to take a moment to consider the Selby Coalfield which caused the 'slicing' referred to above, but yet, in the long sweep of history, is little more than a nine-day wonder.

*A poisonous presence in Bishopwood's leaf litter*

# An interlude : the Selby Coalfield.

This book was written to describe and explain the many historical features that the B1222 passes by and through. But, almost uniquely of any road, it also passes over what was once the future.

I refer to the Selby Coalfield. Although almost entirely forgotten now with almost every physical manifestation of it having been removed from the environment, the Selby Coalfield was once seen as providing energy security for the nation for at least two centuries. An impossible claim? Read the text of the advert from 1979 on the next page to get some idea of quite how vastly important the Coalfield was seen to be half a century ago.

This huge energy resource stretched as far north as the outskirts of York and lay under Selby, Cawood and the entire territory over which we have travelled along the B1222'to date

Writing in the year 2020, but also having lived through the 1960s and 1970s, it is a little challenging to express quite how British life once depended on the coal industry. In the late 1940s, there were over 1500 coal mines distributed across the nation, from Kent to South Wales, through the Midlands, as well as extensive coalfields in Lancashire, Yorkshire, County Durham and southern Scotland. Around 300 000 people worked in these mines. Whilst modernisation had occurred in some pits, in the 1960s, in some mines, coal was still hewn by hand from seams as little as 18 inches high.

The coal won was then used as a major source of electricity generation, domestic and industrial heating and as a feedstock for industry.

When rumours of a massive new coal field under the Vale of York were geologically confirmed in the early 1970s, this was seen as a huge boon for the nation, In the first of many 'political' decisions that were to be linked with the Coalfield, the Wilson Labour Government of 1974-79 pushed forward with rapid development of this resource, employing techniques and methods that mining engineers came from the rest of the world to marvel at. Here was a national resource to be developed for the good of the nation by a nationalised corporation : the National Coal Board (NCB). Here were miners using modern machines in dry, clean conditions, in seams up to 10 feet high. This was - to quote Paul Weller - the 'Modern World'.

Not everyone was in favour locally. Farmers were concerned that subsidence to drainage systems would make their fields sodden. There was concern about building subsidence in the villages. Memorably, one local headmistress looked for police protection for her 'gels' as 'the miners will be involved in drunken fights outside my school gates' Whilst the latter complaint probably didn't get a positive response, most other claims were generously compensated - and since there was so much coal down there, columns of coal could be left under habitations to guard against subsidence.

# Britain has the energy to carry on for at least another 300 years.

We have proven coal resources to last for at least another three hundred years.

Which makes good news when you consider that to replace our present coal output with imported oil would worsen the country's balance of payments by over £5,000,000,000 a year.

And makes especially good news when you remember that world production of oil could well have passed its peak by around the end of the century.

Two good reasons why we should continue to look for coal now.

In fact, exploration is running at ten times the level of ten years ago. And has resulted in some pretty impressive finds.

Selby, in Yorkshire, our biggest new project, will soon be producing its first coal. It will then build-up to ten million tons a year for at least another thirty years.

Which is a lot of coal.

In fact this country now produces as much coal as all the other EEC countries put together.

Not so much coal we can afford to squander it, but not so little that we have to panic.

It simply means British Industry has the time to plan ahead, knowing there is an assured source of energy for at least another three hundred years.

And it gives us lots of time to continue working at maintaining Britain's energy independence. If not directly through coal, then through the conversion of coal into other energy sources, such as oil and gas.

In the technology of using coal, Britain leads the world.

Our most recent breakthrough is known as fluidised bed combustion.

This technique provides higher heat release rates than have been possible with coal up to the present time.

Which means that boiler sizes and therefore capital costs can be reduced.

It also means that, because combustion takes place at a temperature below the melting point of ash, boiler availability is greatly extended, and a wider range of fuels can be burned.

You can seek the advice of our Technical Service experts on fluidised bed combustion, and on other ways of making your plant heating more efficient and more economical.

To discuss your heating needs or problems with an expert, please telephone us.

If you'd simply like to know what coal can offer you, send for a copy of the brochure 'Coal–Your Future'.

Write to the National Coal Board, Technical Service Branch, Marketing Department, Hobart House, Grosvenor Place, London SW1.

Or telephone us on 01-235 2020.

**NCB**

Coal–Britain's energy insurance

*The energy future of the nation assured for centuries to come*
*- as described by a newspaper advertisement of 1979*

As has already been mentioned, the Coalfield caused diversion and closure of the ECML through Naburn, a slicing of acres off Bishopwood in the construction of what became known as the Selby Diversion, and changed the route of the B1222, taking it over a new bridge.

Were these the only consequences, the matter would be a fairly simple one. However, another 'political' question came to the fore.

In the early 1970s, BR was struggling to escape its dingy 1960s decade of line closures, poor services and relatively slow journeys. But just as the Coalfield showed promise of an energy future, so the newly-designed High Speed Train (HST) promised cleaner, quieter and faster journeys. The ECML was clearly a theatre for such modern movement.

But the performance would be spoilt if the HSTs had to wind their way along the curvaceous route via Selby, with the potential of having to wait whilst river bridges at Selby and Naburn were swung against them. Not really the 'Age of the Train'.

But if BR could find a way of avoiding Selby....of running on smart, newly-laid straight track...of using the full potential of the HSTs for 100mph speeds...now that would bring the customers back!

Don't forget, the Coalfield was vast : over 200 years' worth of fuel. If pillars of coal could be left under towns, then why not under a new railway? A great new national energy source and a great new express train : what a vision for Britain in the 1970s!

Evidence at the planning inquiry for the Selby Coalfield was deployed to support this approach. It showed that the locally high water table, and sand substrata would lead to unpredictable subsidence on the Selby to York section of the ECML, and would mean the line was unsafe for a high-speed service. The inquiry recommended that the line be re-sited, as it was said that the alternative of leaving a mile-wide bed of coal underneath the line would mean a loss of £500–800 million. The Parliamentary discussions, which can be followed via Hansard as part of the *British Railways (Selby) Act, 1979*, are uncannily similar to those that have gone on around HS2 40 years later.

Such were the expected profits from the coalfield that a diversionary route for the ECML was built, paid for by the NCB. The NCB proposed this in 1974, and, despite objections from local MPs that it was unnecessarily expensive and would destroy much farmland, following a planning inquiry in 1975, the Selby Diversion received consent in 1976. To allow 125 mph running, the new ECML became the first stretch of rail in this country designed for such a speed.

The entire line, amounting to almost 14 miles of new track was completed in three years, opening three months ahead of schedule. It was formally opened for all services on Oct 3rd 1983, but had been open for local diesel multiple units and driver training for several months before that. At this date, the line north from Selby to York, that served Naburn, was officially closed. The cost was estimated at £60 million, the bulk given over to engineering works.

## The Selby Coalfield Diversion (SCD) (much simplified)

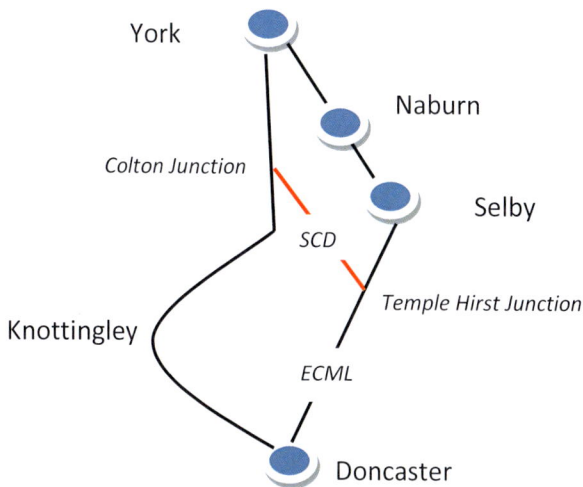

The future had arrived! The line via Knottingley was of poor quality with many junctions : not ideal for the new HSTs. The ECML via Naburn? Potential delays due to river swing bridges : not ideal for HSTs either. The Selby Diversion was free of both problems  Ideal for HSTs!!

Did BR have the new, modern services they desired? The brochure linked to the launch of the service makes it clear : "The HST is the most significant event on the Edinburgh-Newcastle-London main line for decades. It will provide a standard no other railway in the world will offer you."

And how about the NCB and a source of cheap energy until the year 2200? As we all know, politics played a further role with the Miners' Strike of 1984/5. Subsequently, geological problems and ingress of water meant that extracting the coal was neither as easy nor as profitable as many had expected. By the 1990s, the nation and the world had found cleaner and cheaper energy resources, and King Coal had been toppled from his throne. The Selby Coalfield did produce record-breaking amounts of coal, but its time had gone. The final coal extraction from the Selby complex occurred in 2004, and, since then, almost every sign of the existence of pits in the quiet Vale of York has been expunged.

In 2020, the straightened and gracefully-bridged B1222 at Bishopwood is, arguably, one of the few extant reminders, apart from the stretch of the 'new' , high-speed ECML,  of this great, lost British Civil Engineering project.

But enough of 'could have beens' and 'should have beens'. It is time to leave transport and energy politics behind and return to our road's historical route.

*Long-gone traces of the Selby Coalfield.*

T junction to Wistow Mine off the B1222 at Long Lane between Cawood and Sherburn (above) and the modern (but now demolished) pithead viewed from the Cawood turn off along Long Lane (below).

# Transit 7 : Bishopwood to Sherburn in Elmet

Having read about the coalfield, a reminder. To return to the B1222 follow Scalm Lane, over the ECML and then carefully turn left at the junction to transit towards Sherburn.

This transit has a mixture of what could be described as forgotten lands and modern technology. To save hopping between one and the other, each category is described separately, although as part of a journey, they are mixed together. So perhaps you need to read all the detail before setting out, and a sketch map - as below - will hopefully help.

Your reward at the end of the transit is to enter a kingdom whose roots lie at the very start of our Anglo-Saxon history. More detail of the B1222's doings will recommence at the first roundabout on the entrance to Sherburn.

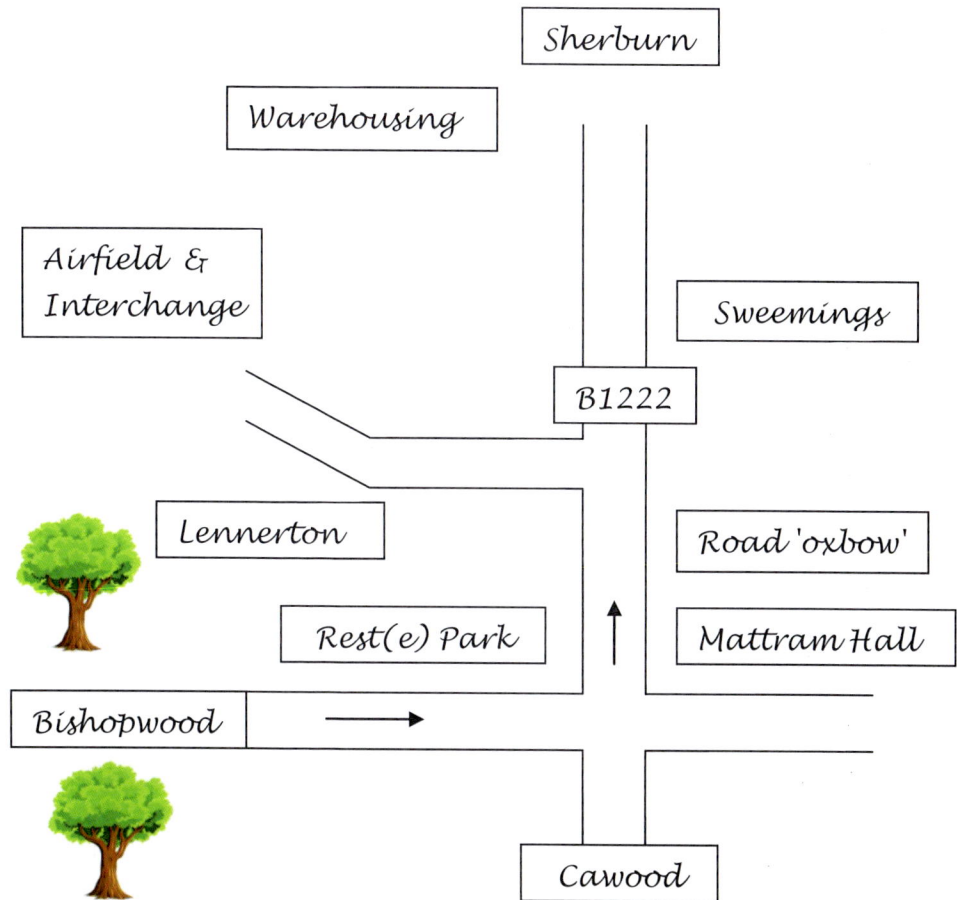

# Forgotten lands

As we approach the crossroads, the area to our left is the site of Rest(e) Park, described as being *"fields in the neighbourhood of Manor Garth now only a system of moats but clearly the site in former times of a substantial habitation"*. A 13th century deer park for the Archbishops of York with a manor house became farmland with traces of these earlier buildings removed by 1970.

On the far side of the road was the site of Mattram Hall, formerly containing a hospital set up by the Vavasour family of nearby Hazlewood Castle, but now a farmhouse and fields.

A little further along on the right there are a few houses which comprise the hamlet of North Sweeming, and as the road once again crosses Bishopdyke, the site of Sweeming Bridge.

Those who know their word history say that this name reflects that it was an old habitation on a slight rise, in other words, a mound that was burnt down or 'svided'. Smash the two words together to get 'Svide - mund' and allow a few hundred years of Yorkshire dialect-speak to round it off to 'Sweeming', All this mounding and burning may have taken place at the site of a small castle just across the dyke, but details, as you may guess, are sketchy in the extreme.

Conversely, something that is very solid is a small house and yard on the right of the road at a bend. This is the former Half Moon Inn, once grand enough to feature in a 1960s publication, 'Inns of Character of the West Riding', as shown below. It is perhaps a shame that the house is no longer a public one, as the chance to take in Mr. Whittaker's highly individual approach to bar decoration would surely be a highlight for any modern pub-goer.

**HALF MOON INN,
LENNERTON, SHERBURN-IN-ELMET.**

Map Ref. 72.

Four years ago when Mr. Whittaker, the present proprietor, took over the Half-Moon it was rather a neglected place. Since then his many improvements have created a splendid little Inn that is situated two miles on the B1222 road east of Sherburn-in-Elmet.

Painted around the walls of the lounge is a mural depicting the Feast of Bacchus. Soft music from hidden speakers permeates the rooms and combined with discreet lighting goes to make a restful atmosphere. The central bar, which is partitioned by a display stand, serves the lounge and public room.

FREE HOUSE.

D.B. Wor. Melbourne. Young.

The beers on offer will cause the taste buds of more seasoned drinkers some sadness.

Melbourne of Leeds was absorbed by Tetley's in the early1960s, Worthington by Bass at a similar time and Young might refer to products of the former Albion Brewery of Leeds (and not the South London firm)

'DB'? Draught Beer, of course : the guide was written when the modern concept of effort-free, non-living cask ale was the new thing, and the Campaign for Real Ale but a far-off dream.

Also in this area notice on the right a 'cut off' piece of road, like an oxbow lake, and a concrete platform next to Bishopdyke. This presumably was some kind of loading staithe.

## Modern Technology

### Gascoigne Wood/Sherburn Rail Freight Distribution Centre

New Lennerton Lane lies off to the left of the B1222, harking back to possibly Viking times when this area was 'Leofnoth's farm'.

A side trip along the lane allows access to two much more modern artefacts : a distribution centre and an airfield. Firstly, another relic of the Selby Coalfield. Whilst it would be incorrect to say that no expense was spared in developing the project, it is clear that every effort was made to ensure that the project was as modern as possible. This modernism extended to the way in which the coal was to be taken away from the site. No grimy coal yards, mucky coal hoists and dirty trucks taking the black stuff away. No. All product was funnelled by underground means to the centre at Gascoigne Wood where it would be fed by conveyor belt into fleets of waiting coal trucks that were ready and waiting in an ample provision of sidings. All would be overseen by a modern signalling box and marshalling control tower central to the yard.

Whilst the coalfield was in production, this was a fine thing. However, on final closure of the pits in 2004, its purpose vanished overnight. In the subsequent years buildings have decayed and been demolished. Sidings have rusted. The owners of the site have searched for new uses : a rail freight distribution hub, and the centre for a new 'eco town' being just two. Signs along the B1222 continue to refer to 'Sherburn Rail Distribution Centre' or 'Gascoigne Wood Interchange'. Sadly, little seems to have come of any of these ventures and to the casual eye all the hopes and aspirations of the 1970s are being left to slowly rot away. It is very clear from the extent of fencing and signage that casual access to inspect these remains is strongly discouraged. Rail travellers on services between Leeds and Selby pass through the centre of this dereliction. Some rail-based freight work concerning aggregate movement looks to be ongoing, but overall, it is a very melancholy sight.

Much better to return to the road and continue to the more welcoming ambience of the Aero Club.

# Sherburn Aero Club

The jumble of industrial buildings, and, at the time of writing in late 2020, several fields full of new cars awaiting delivery are some of the uses of the grounds of what was once Sherburn Airfield and now the premises of the Sherburn Aero Club. There is more than a century of flying history in the Sherburn area, starting as early as 1911.

A group of aerial enthusiasts, including Leeds lad Robert Blackburn, were probably using fields to the west of the present airfield as early as 1911, and in the First World War the field was commandeered by the Armed Forces. By 1918 it covered 177 acres, with 8 hangars, 21 storage sheds and various other structures.

Sherburn airfield was used as an Aircraft Acceptance Park for aircraft manufactured at Blackburn's Olympia works in Leeds. On the Sherburn site, Blackburn's constructed many First World War 'planes, including an order to build the torpedo-bearing craft, the Sopwith Cuckoo under license. After the war, the RAF ceased to use the airfield but Blackburn's retained workshops.

Blackburn's went on to build the rather more famous factory at Brough and the company continued in business until taken over by Hawker Siddeley in 1963.

Returning to the story at Sherburn, the Yorkshire Aeroplane Club became based at Sherburn in 1926, with a clubhouse following in 1928. The new pastime of flying was hugely popular, and an air pageant in summer 1926 drew over 5000 people to the airfield. The author Neville Shute was an early member of the club.

During 1934 Sherburn was used as a terminus for a twice daily Leeds – Paris air service. At the start of World War 2 in 1939, the airfield and the club's aircraft were pressed into military service. The Blackburn buildings were used to construct warplanes, the most well-known of which was the Fairey Swordfish, of which almost 2000 were built. In an echo of the First World War provision, these were also torpedo-launching 'planes. The field itself was mainly used as a storage area and a point from which planes were delivered to other airfields. This ceased with the end of the war. On site aircraft construction also ceased.

If you stop off to tour Sherburn, you'll see a small memorial to the Blackburn factory and its workers, in the form of a sculpture of a 'Swordfish' 'plane, as illustrated on page 93.

After the war, flying for pleasure gradually returned, and an international rally and air races were staged in 1950, attracting, it is said, 30 000 spectators.

The club attached to the airfield has had its ups and downs since the 1950s, but still exists today and the clubhouse remains open to the public.

# Forgotten kingdoms : What was 'Elmet' ?

Having considered vanished settlements, tiny hamlets and 20th. century technology, it is now time to consider the Anglo Saxon realm of Elmet.

Elmet was one of a number of sub-Roman realms in what is now northern England that existed in the final years of the Roman occupation, and before the Angles, Saxons and Jutes came across from the continent. 'Elmet' seems to be derived from Welsh roots, but no actual meaning is obtained. Reference to works of the Venerable Bede imply it might be 'Elm wood'. The first recorded 'leader' of Elmet is the intriguingly titled Mascuid the Lame, dating from the mid fifth century. Elmet may have been created as a geopolitically- defensive move by Masuid's father who then put him in command.

What elevates Elmet's story from being a footnote in the early history of these islands is the fact that the kingdom was the final Celtic stronghold against the Anglo Saxons, sustaining a kind of early medieval Celtic 'M62' corridor across the Pennines towards North Wales, between two Anglo Saxon kingdoms.

***Tribal England around 600 AD.***

*The Celtic kingdoms are the ones in boxes. Elmet is the only Celtic territory that allows safe and easy passage of the Celts in the west to the North Sea. This explains Elmet's strategic importance and why its defeat meant the domestic cultural development of what became England was entirely Anglo Saxon.*

After 200 years or so of independent existence, towards the end of the 6th century, Elmet came under increasing pressure from the expanding Anglo-Saxon kingdoms of Deira to the north-east, Bernicia to the north and Mercia to the south. After the unification of Deira and Bernicia to form Northumbria, the Northumbrians invaded and overran Elmet in 616 or 617 AD, expelling the final ruler, Ceretic or Cerdic. Brown, in his book, (see references)suggests Elmet's final stand may have been at Grim's ditch near Thorner. Parts of this defensive earthwork remain near Swillington. Others suggest a final battle at Bawtry near Doncaster.

Elmet's boundaries are uncertain but are assumed to be linked to rivers. The Sheaf (of Sheffield fame) to the south. the Wharfe (Ilkley and Tadcaster) to the north and east and the Calder (Halifax, Huddersfield) to the west. It is possible that the capital of Elmet was Leeds, although it is also thought that the 'moots' or tribal gatherings were held at the Ash Tree at nearby Barkston Ash, which is still noted as being the geographic centre of Yorkshire's ancient Ridings.

This romantic image of 'Elmet' has provided literary inspiration. The former Poet Laureate, Ted Hughes, composed a book of poetry, 'Remains of Elmet', in which he refers to Elmet as being 'a more or less uninhabitable wilderness, a notorious refuge for criminals, a hide-out for refugees'. Before Sherburn-ites get too restive about Ted's opinions, he was referring to the part of Elmet in the Calder Valley above Halifax.

The suffix '-in Elmet' is also shared today by the nearby villages of Barwick and Scholes, and the local Parliamentary constituency is deemed Elmet and Rothwell. In earlier times, the suffix was used by the West Yorkshire townships of Burton Salmon, Clifford, High Melton, Kirkby Wharfe, Micklefield, Saxton, South Kirkby and Sutton. The map on the next page, shows the spread of these settlements.

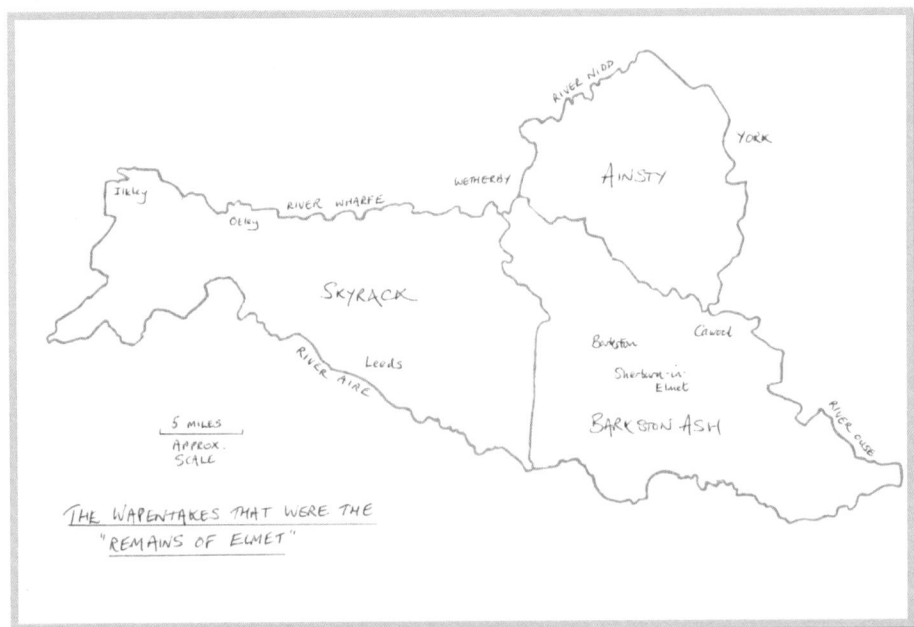

*The three Wapentakes or Anglo-Saxon administrative units that Elmet may have been reduced to after the Northumbrian conquest (after the map in Brown's book, p.14 : see reference section)*

For four centuries following Ceretic's expulsion, the Celtic people of Elmet seem to have resigned themselves to remain in the area and 'rolled with the flow', accepting either Anglo Saxon or Viking rule, depending on the vagaries of battles fought elsewhere.

At some time in this Viking/Saxon period, the name 'Scireburn' ,meaning 'bright stream', is recorded, from which it is said 'Sherburn' derives. There are, however, no obvious candidates for such a 'bright stream' today.

Evidence for Elmet's longevity comes from a document in Florence, Italy, dating from around 1315 which records that wool coming 'd'Elmetta' ('from Elmet') is worth 11 marks per sack : cheaper than Leeds' wares, but more expensive than those from Thirsk or York.

Although it has now been fourteen centuries since the Celts were overcome their influence is still apparently to be found in genetics. DNA research in 2015 showed that residents in and around the old area of Elmet maintain a different genetic composition to those in the rest of Yorkshire.

As we travel along the B1222 we are therefore approaching a major settlement of a people with a long and proud history.

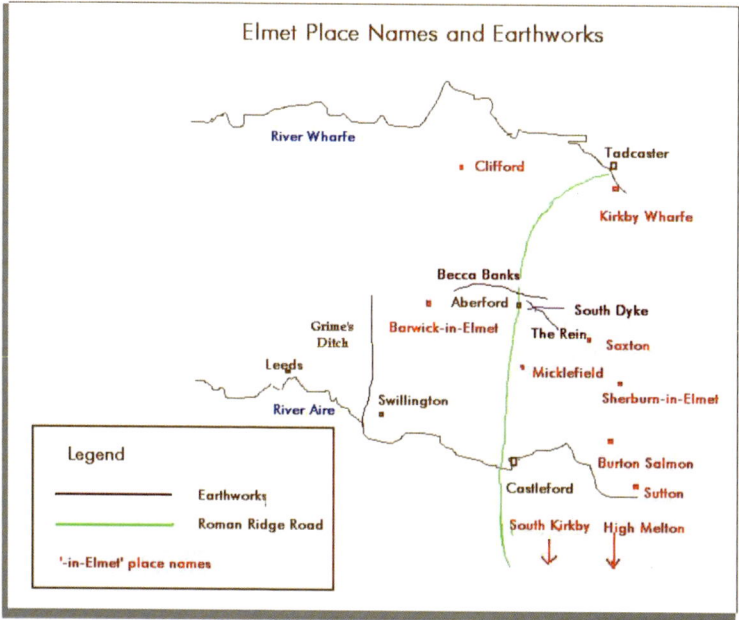

Elmet Place Names and Earthworks

River Wharfe

Clifford

Tadcaster

Kirkby Wharfe

Becca Banks

Aberford

South Dyke

Grime's Ditch

Barwick-in-Elmet

The Rein

Saxton

Leeds

Micklefield

Swillington

Sherburn-in-Elmet

River Aire

Burton Salmon

Castleford

Sutton

South Kirkby

High Melton

Legend

———————— Earthworks

———————— Roman Ridge Road

'-in-Elmet' place names

*This map, and that of Tribal England, courtesy of Barwick in Elmet Historical Society*

# Tour 8 : Sherburn in Elmet

*The commemorative statue to the Blackburn Aircraft factory on Low Street*

Having established the importance of the 'in Elmet' suffix, to save space, I'll just refer to 'Sherburn' for the rest of this tour. Also, some say that Sherburn is one of the largest villages in Yorkshire : but to me it feels more like a town, so I trust Elmet-ites will take it as a compliment if I refer to it as such.

The arrival by road or rail into a place of such historical import is hardly auspicious. By road, modern distribution depots to our left and a 21st century roundabout make up the welcoming party. The roundabout is another diversion of the B1222 from its former path. Rather as on the approaches to Cawood from Stillingfleet, the original line of the B1222 can be seen veering off to the right where it now ultimately leads just to the railway station. The station itself is a simple two-platform affair, with the minimum of facilities: but it is a rare example of a re-opening after a Beeching closure. Closed in 1965, it was re-opened in a joint venture between British Rail and the local councils in 1985. It has a modest level of services, largely to York, Selby and Hull, with around 60 000 passenger journeys recorded per year.

*The old course of the B1222, at Sherburn Station level crossing, approaching Sherburn from Cawood*

Walking across the former level crossing, the line of the road into Sherburn can be seen, past a pub and a row of terraced houses. This former part of the B1222 has yet another name : Oak Terrace.

The new course of the B1222 has taken it straight on and over the railway line, before dropping down to a second roundabout, where the Sherburn by pass, constructed in the 1990s, intersects with our road. Just beyond this point, the Bishopdyke parts company from the close association with the B1222 it has maintained since Cawood, and strikes a course right, next to the Sherburn by pass that has inherited the designation "A162", past the new housing estates before petering out in Barkston Ash. The B1222 has been intermittently described as 'Bishopdyke Road' since Cawood, and on older maps, but now becomes 'Moor Lane', referring to the moorland crossed on the approach to Sherburn.

The original and new B1222's continue to a mini roundabout, where they coalesce. The road then continues through housing developments of various 20th century vintages towards the centre of Sherburn. At the traffic lights, the B1222 dog-legs across Low Street, the local name of what was once the A162. Running north /south along the line of the old Great North Road between Darrington and Tadcaster, Low Street was part of the route along which the Mails and important passengers travelled between London and York.

*The view down Low Street, from Finkle Hill  The 'Red Bear' is to the right in the middle distance.*

Looking down Low Street, the width of the road and the variety of inns, with arches wide enough for a coach, and yards capacious enough for good stabling, tell of an earlier kind of transport. The road was a turnpike and coaches would halt for refreshment, deposit or collection of passengers, goods or mail and perhaps fresh motive power. Only five miles away, the B1222 crossed the railway, the modern way to the north: now here it is doing the same with the 18th century version.  We have now arrived in the centre of Sherburn, and should you wish to explore, turn either left or right at the traffic lights to find car parks.

For the purposes of the tour, let's assume you've gone right at the lights to the car park at the top of Finkle Hill. There is an old saw that says 'finkle' derives from the Norse 'vinkle' meaning an elbow, implying any highway bearing such a name would be bent.  The fact that Finkle Hill is arrow-straight here rather demolishes the theory!

Our tour of Sherburn begins at the car park at the top of Finkle Hill. The map on the next page illustrates it,

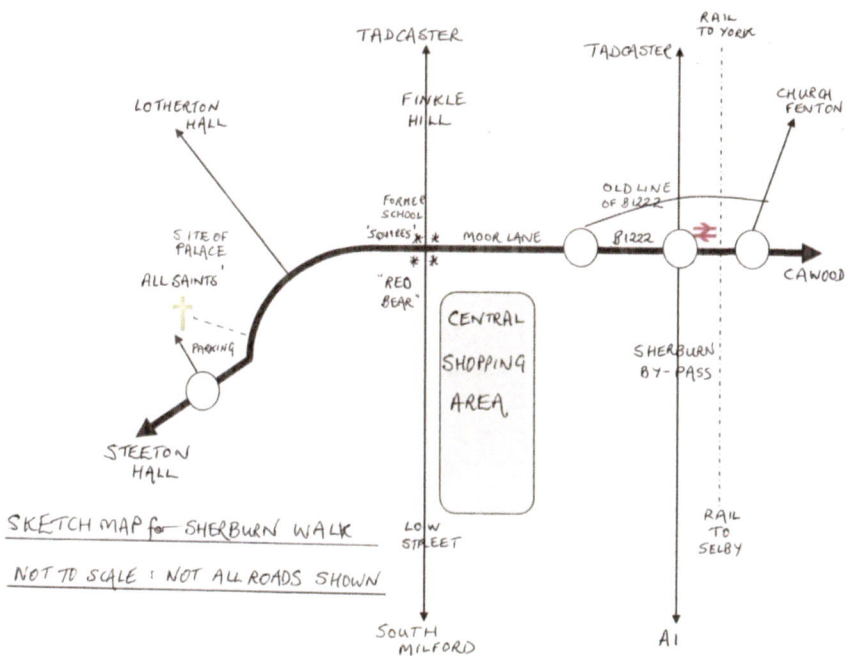

SKETCH MAP for SHERBURN WALK

NOT TO SCALE : NOT ALL ROADS SHOWN

Map labels: TADCASTER, RAIL TO YORK, TADCASTER, CHURCH FENTON, LOTHERTON HALL, FINKLE HILL, FORMER SCHOOL, "SQUIRES", MOOR LANE, OLD LINE OF B1222, B1222, SITE OF PALACE, ALL SAINTS, "RED BEAR", CENTRAL SHOPPING AREA, SHERBURN BY-PASS, CAWOOD, PARKING, STEETON HALL, LOW STREET, RAIL TO SELBY, SOUTH MILFORD, A1

Walking down Finkle Hill into town, at the crossroads there is an imposing grey building with a coat of arms over the main entrance. This is the former Old Boys' or Hungate School.

The name links back to a bequest in the will of local landowner Robert Hungate, who died in 1619, for the provision of a school. We may think that education authorities move slowly these days : but back in the 17th century, it was not until 31 years later, in 1650, that there are records of lessons being taught - to boys only. The school closed when the new Sherburn Hungate school opened, back up the hill, behind the Co-Op. The building was then used as a community centre and is now a medical hub.

Having crossed the B1222 at the traffic lights, on the same side as the Hungate building is a fine old coaching inn, the Red Bear. This was the main coaching inn in the village and the place where the London to Edinburgh mail coaches changed horses on the stage from Ferrybridge to Tadcaster. To the rear of the Inn an extensive yard of stables catered for the needs of the mail coach motive power. The Red Bear also was the venue for a court that presided over local petty sessions. The external stonework of the Inn has been scrupulously cleaned and a fine new sign, similar to the 19th century one hangs above the main entrance. The façade is a fine example of local stone used well in an important town-centre building.

THE RED BEAR INN, SHERBURN.

*The 'Red Bear' circa 1870 (above) and 2020 (below)*

If you continue down Low Street, you come to the sculpture that commemorates the achievements of the Blackburn factory as referred to on page 89. Across the minor road, the town's rich and varied commercial and social history is outlined on a three-sided information board that describes the saucy story of Eversley Park. Music, drama and religion all get a mention; food, fabric and farming are all weighed up and three royal interventions in Sherburn's affairs are detailed.

But, being a place that gives the air of wishing to concentrate on present commerce and future expansion rather than past glories, there are few extant reminders of this varied past.

This area of Sherburn contains a fine mixture of independent and multiple stores, sufficient for most needs. Strolling further along Low Street, the names of streets to either side show that there were once something other than houses here: Orchard Cottages and Cricketers' Way being two obvious examples.

As the commercial centre of the town is left behind, on the right is the Eversley Park Centre, the modern successor of the Eversley Park estate mentioned at the information boards. Across the road is a renovated example of the kind of distance-marking stones that were a common sight along turnpike roads. Were you to continue along Low Street it would become 'London Road' , an Anglicised example of the old saying that 'all roads lead to Rome'. But that would take us away from our road, so time to retrace our steps to the B1222.

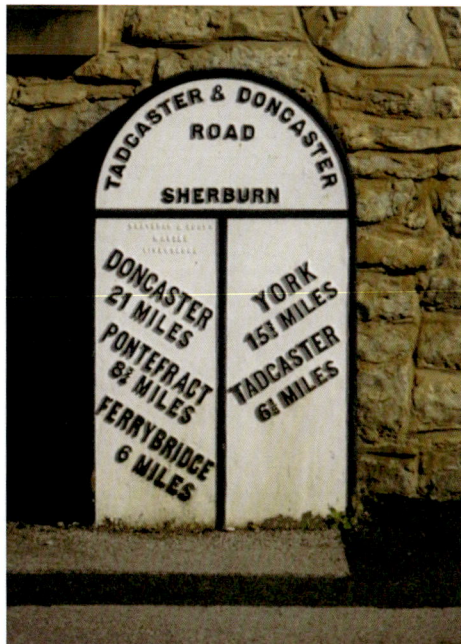

Returning to the traffic-light junction, turn left to discover ancient and modern reasons for Sherburn's historical importance. Going uphill, the B1222 undergoes yet another name change, now being called 'Kirkgate'.

The Viking suffix -'gata' or gate effectively meaning 'road towards' and 'Kirk' is 'church'. All Saints' church is indeed to be found along Kirkgate, which is where the ancient history lies, but first there's a now-invisible modern matter to deal with.

*Mileage marker on Low Street*

On the right, an innocuous looking block of modern flats sits on the site of a leather-jacketed legend. For here was the site of a fabled motorcyclists' Mecca, Squires Milk Bar. Fuller details are on page 103 but suffice to say that, twice a week, for over 40 years, biking fans from across the nation met here.

*'Squires" café bar, Kirkgate on its final evening, 2002.(courtesy Sherburn Local History Soc.)*

Continuing the rise out of Sherburn, the former Girls;' High School, now a community centre is passed before, at Sir John's Lane, the B1222 undergoes another name change. From Norse 'Kirkgate' the road becomes its modern Anglicized variant 'Church Hill' at 'Cowbell Corner'. This name harks back to the 'Tour de Yorkshire' of 2017. To mark that event, a 'Sherburn Cycle Saturday' was organised and massed crowds gathered here to spur on their lycra-clad heroes with a salvo of sound from cowbells supplied by the local Scouts.

All Saints' Church commands the scene to your right, but to enjoy a full tour, follow the road as it curves, ignoring the path through the church wall adjacent to the war memorial. When you get to a mini roundabout bear right and go uphill. Bordering the car park is a stone wall with eroded carved inserts. One such shows five diamonds in a diagonal line, the mark of the de Reygate family of Steeton Hall (see page 107).

The main entrance to All Saints' Church lies ahead, with a porch added as part of the 1857 renovations. To the right of the porch is part of a Saxon preaching cross. A church on this site certainly existed in Saxon times, replaced around 1110 AD by a Norman building, which forms the core of today's structure.

The church is often open, with helpful volunteers and a range of informative leaflets. If you are able to enter, another example of the five diagonal de Reygate diamonds are carved into the left hand wall. Inside there are massive round pillars in the nave, similar in design to ones in Selby Abbey and Durham Cathedral, decorated Norman arches and some fine stained glass. A simple model of the 12th. century building is on show.

*Janus Cross inside All Saints'*

One unique item on display is the so-called 'Janus Cross' dating from the 15th century. Janus was the Roman god of doorways, and so a religious icon that had images on both sides could be called a Janus Cross. The story goes that such a cross was discovered on the site of a derelict chapel inside the church grounds. However, there was a dispute as to who owned it: the vicar or the churchwarden.

To resolve the matter, in a mighty example of sawmanship, the cross was sawn in half lengthwise. The church kept one half : the other was displayed where the churchwarden lived, at nearby Steeton Hall (see page 105). Thankfully the matter was eventually resolved and both halves returned to the church around the turn of the 20th century. The de Reygate diamonds are in evidence yet again, underneath the cross.

Having enjoyed, if possible, the interior of All Saints', walk to the rear of the church to inspect possibly the most important royal aspect of the B1222's journey. You are presented with an imposing view of flat land stretching to York Minster on the skyline, and a *The* bench, kindly provided by the local WI, to rest awhile as you take it all in.

It is not surprising that a site with such a commanding view has seen important uses. The location was a base for King Athelstan (895-939). Described by historian Michael Wood as '*the most powerful ruler in England since the Romans*', Athelstan was the grandson of Alfred the Great, and King of the Saxons from 924-927, in which time he established Saxon superiority over Wessex, Mercia and Northumbria, and finally overthrowing the Scandinavian kingdom of York in 927, becoming the first king to have control over all of the English.

In 937 he defeated an alliance of Scots and Scandinavians at the Battle of Brunanburh, to become "*Rex Totius Britannia*" : King of all Britain, a legend he had stamped on his coins. As one instance of thanks for this victory he gave the manors at Sherburn and Cawood to the Archbishop of York.

In trading terms, he effectively established the concept of a market town, strengthened the nation's currency and, geopolitically, established links across Europe by marrying off his sisters to appropriate Continental nobles. Medieval historian Dr. Veronica Ortenberg described Athelstan as '*The most powerful ruler in Europe*'. Quite a reputation to have established in a dozen or so years!

*All Saints' Sherburn, overlooking part of the site of "Athelstan's Palace"*

Marked on older maps as 'Hall Garth', the land facing north in the angle between the B1222 and Sir John's Lane is the site of Athelstan's palace. A small modern road, "Hall Garth Mews" is nearby. Today the area is deemed a Scheduled Monument of national importance due to its association with Athelstan and four subsequent centuries of use by the Archbishops of York.

A 'palace' like Athelstan's typically consisted of many timber buildings, the most prominent being a large "Great Hall", with smaller additional administrative structures around it. Being wooden, these rarely survive to modern times. Any stone buildings would have had their material re-used when the site was abandoned. What may survive from the early tenth century occupation are foundation trenches, post holes for timber buildings and rubbish pits.

The site today consists of a number of earthworks including the lines of walls, up to 50cm high; ditches up to 6 metres wide, terraces and small quarrying areas up to 4 metres wide. Anglo-Saxon occupation around the site was probably more extensive than the area bounded by the current confines, but its extent is uncertain. There is no opportunity to investigate what is little more than a bumpy field, as access is currently not allowed.

The palace buildings and site were subsequently used as a hunting lodge by the Archbishops, but by 1361, it had all fallen into ruin and the Archbishop of the time, John Thoresby, ordered demolition.

Stone from the palace was later used in the building of the Choir at York Minster as well as in the construction of Rest Park - the site of which was passed near Bishopwood.

Having completed the tour, return towards the front of the church and take the stoned path down the slope to the War Memorial. Go left as you meet the B1222 once more and thence back downhill towards the town centre.

*Remnant of the Saxon cross (left) and Sherburn's War Memorial (right)*

# Transit 8 : Sherburn to Steeton Hall Gateway via Squires'

It is now time to return to the road, and visit a stretch of road that might, observing the users of the highway, make you think you were on the Isle of Man. For we are in the realm of that fabled motorbike Mecca, Squires café bar. The Sherburn to Leeds bus, boarding on Low Street, will also take you along this section of the B1222, and the top deck gives a panoramic view.

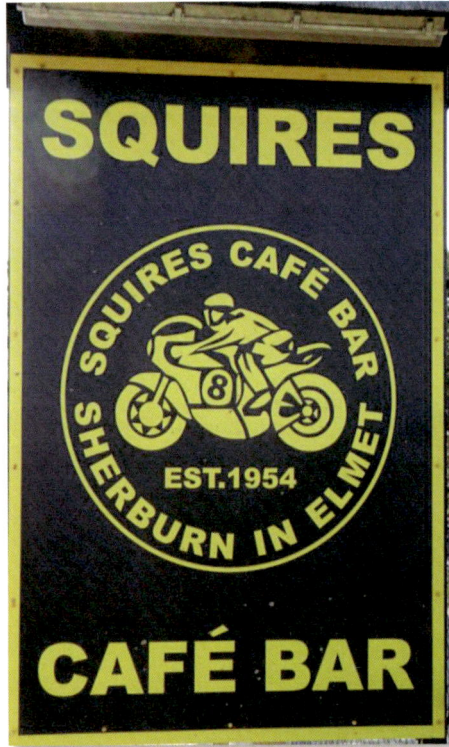

*Squires' sign on the B1222, and a modest collection of 'bikes and riders, with car park to left and Leeds/Selby railway in the background.*

103

On leaving Sherburn, the road now gently rises and then continues on its characteristic curvy course as it passes through farmland. Old maps show that there are many disused quarries to either side of the road and it was from such quarries that stone was sent along the Bishopdyke. Entering the parish of Newthorpe, the famed Huddlestone quarries - suppliers of stone to York Minster and Selby Abbey - are to the right.

The road now dives under another railway line : this one linking Leeds, Selby and Hull. The Leeds to Selby section can proudly be described as 'Yorkshire's First Main Line' , opening in September 1834. The stonework of the skew-arch bridge is of the characteristic high quality applied to all the engineering works between Leeds and Selby. **Close inspection of this is not advised**, however, as much is hidden behind modern concrete, there are no footpaths and the road approaches the bridge via blind bends.

Directly after the bridge, in the grounds of the former 'New Inn' you'll almost certainly see a gaggle of motor bikes. This is the new site of 'Squires' café, referred to in the Sherburn tour.

From 1954 until 2002 'Squires Bradbury's Milk Bar' on Kirkgate in Sherburn was a legendary venue in the motorcycling world.

Bikers travelled to 'Squires' from all parts of the UK, traditionally meeting on a Wednesday evening or Sunday afternoon. These weekly meets were a remarkable sight: motorbikes of all ages, makes and sizes congregating around Squires to enjoy chat, soft drinks and snacks and, of course, a rock'n'roll jukebox. Whilst the meets did cause a degree of disturbance to the local community, by and large, relations remained harmonious.

In 1974, original owner Squires Bradbury sold up and the cafe was taken over by Harry and Sue Weston, regulars since 1961. With the ever increasing popularity of the café, and larger meets also happening at weekends, it was clear that things were outgrowing a town-centre base. The New Inn at Newthorpe, some 5 miles along the B1222 became available, and in 2002 the move to more spacious surroundings was made. This gave the bikers more space and town residents more peace and quiet. Everyone won.

Squires' cafe has now developed far beyond anything that could have been envisaged at the original Sherburn town centre site. Free car parking is available in front of the former pub - but this is usually crowded, so it is easier to use the field to the right.

If you're a fan of motor bikes, all manner of machines are usually on display here and their riders are often ready to chat about them and their exploits on the B1222 and further afield.

Leave 'Squires' behind and press on through gentle, rural, limestone countryside, but fairly soon, one final attraction presents itself. About half a mile from Squires, tiny Whitecote Lane veers off sharply to the left, signposted 'South Milford'. A mile or so along it, on the right, is one of English Heritage's smaller properties, Steeton Hall Gateway.

# Tour 9 : Steeton Hall Gateway

*The Gateway itself, The vaulted ceiling (left) and a beastly corbel*

The name Steeton apparently implies a farmstead amongst tree stumps. Several candidates that may have been responsible for such a name can be seen in the locality, but it is the fine medieval gateway that we have come to see.

There is no charge, and no property per se to visit - just the chance to admire the exterior of a 14th-century gateway. But this is no ordinary gateway. It is Grade I listed, the highest level possible, defined as being 'a building of exceptional interest'. You are therefore visiting a structure of equal heritage status to Tower Bridge and York Minster.

So why is this gateway, probably built more for display than defence, of such status? Initial impressions are striking : a fine wide arch for carriage access, a narrower one for pedestrians, and on the first floor, overlooking it all, a room for a porter or gatekeeper. The passage through to the rear of the gateway displays the quality of the construction. The Yorkshire Archaeological Society ('YAS') article referred to in the reference section describes the underside of the carriage arch as 'a large and loftier gate . . . ceiled with a quadripartite ribbed vault'. The stonework is excellent. There is a fine and unusual octagonal chimney. There are fine and dramatic battlements.

But the star attraction here are the corbels. These are the stone supports that mainly support the battlements. At Steeton, there are 54 of them - some human, some animal, some heraldic. Some are lifelike and some veer towards fantasy or the grotesquery of a gargoyle. Whilst weathering has taken its toll on the fine detail of the carving, they are still worth inspection, and a pair of binoculars will help.

As well as giving an insight into the history of the gateway, it is interesting to compare the 14th century style of carvings here with the 12th century techniques on display at St. Helen's in Stillingfleet.

*A human head underneath an eroded water spout, flanked by heraldic devices.*

The left hand shield is described, in heraldic terms as "*three mullets of six points, two and one, over all a canton*" A mullet is not a reference to 1980s hairstyles, but in heraldic terms is a six-pointed star. A canton is a square taking up the top left corner (as one looks at it) of the shield. The YAS article states this is perhaps the heraldic device of the Harengill family, of whom little seems to be known.

The badge to the right is "*A chevron between three hinds' heads, couped*". 'Couped' implies as if the heads have been cut off the neck of the creature. YAS tell us this may well be the badge of the Malbis family, whose name derives from the Norman Malbysse or De Malebys meaning 'very swarthy'. Here is a possible link back to an earlier part of the B1222 odyssey.

The village of Acaster Malbis lies close to the B1222, a little further downstream and on the opposite side of the river at Naburn. "Acaster" implies a camp, so perhaps some swarthy invading Normans camped close to the B1222 on their way to harry the North!

Many other fascinating stories lie hidden behind the heraldry, but the final one to mention is of the family for whom the Gateway was constructed, the de Reygates.

Their device was five narrow diamonds or lozenges along a diagonal, or, as the heraldic world puts it "*five fusils in bend, an annulet for difference*".

This is the Reygate badge, but having an 'annulet (or ring) for difference' implies that it was not the head of the household who was responsible for the final building. The fact that the fusils are on an oval shield implies that these are the arms of a woman. This all suggests that whilst father William de Reygate began the construction, it was only completed under the authority of his daughter Elizabeth after William's death in 1367.

*The de Reygate diamonds*

The badge can also be seen in the porch of All Saints' at Sherburn, and underneath the Janus Cross, probably denoting the time that the cross spent here.

William had gained his status and his fortune by being an escheator or financial administrator for King Edward III in the county of York. An escheator dealt with property rights after a death, so whilst the job may have been burdensome, it was also potentially lucrative.

Looking at the Hall that remains and the lands and the stone walls it's easy to imagine a prosperous estate here. One's imagination could plausibly stretch further to imagine William and noble guests riding down to his house from business in York, and riding out to hunt in Bishopwood. Whilst it is pleasant to indulge in such flights of fancy, all apart from the Gateway structure is private, so no further exploration is possible.

Therefore, it is time to retrace your path to return to the B1222. On reaching the junction, turn left for the final mile of the B1222's journey.

# Transit 9 : Steeton Hall Gateway to the End of the Road

This is a very short transit : from Whitecote Lane to the point at which the B1222 joins what was the A1 and is now the A63. It may be possible to pick up the Sherburn - Leeds bus at the end of Whitecote Lane to travel this section.

The transit still has significance. In its journey, the B1222 has had cause to cross the 19th. century north-south rail route, the 21st century version of the same thing and a major coaching highway covering the same journey. In its final half mile, it crosses both the 21st century north-south road route, and passes under its 20th century predecessor. In the introduction to the book, I pointed out how B roads were 'link' roads taking traffic to and from villages to major trunk routes. In its 20-mile length, the B1222 has clearly carried out many such links..

By the middle of the 2000's the original A1 road had reached its capacity and beyond, so an entirely new course for what is now the A1(M) was created. It is this new road that the B1222 crosses. The A1(M) runs beneath through a limestone cutting showing traces of the pale yellow stone that for centuries was quarried locally : some of which was taken along the Bishopdyke.

In a manner reminiscent of the B1222's swoop over the A64 at Fulford and the ECML at Bishopwood, the B1222 is now directed over the A1(M). Just before this swoop a final stretch of 'original' B1222 goes off to the right. This is now merely a farm track . On the far side of the A1(M) the other half of this 'original' road eventually trails back into the new path of the B1222 as it all ends up in the junctions described in the following section. As the B1222 approaches what was the Great North Road, but is now the A63, its direct course is divided. To go south, branch to the left. To go north, continue straight ahead, under the old A1, a diversion itself created to increase capacity in the early 1960s, as our final tour describes.

*The B1222, looking back towards Sherburn, passing under the A1 bridge of the 1960s.*

# The End of the Road

*Southbound A63/A1, former B1222 slip road east (right) and current one north (in shadow) (left)*

At the eastern terminus of the B1222, the junction of B1222 and A19 is a simple T junction. At this western end, things are more complex.

When I began my research on the book, sites dedicated to roads described the B1222 as running from Fulford to the 'Boot and Shoe' pub, in Garforth, on the old A1. (Please note, in this chapter 'A1' means the 'old A1' - not the new one in the cutting you've just crossed over). It's not unusual to refer to a pub as a destination : in the days before we all trusted in satnavs, an instruction like *'Turn left at the White Horse and the football ground is on the right by the Three Magpies'* would have been clearly understood. A few such geographic descriptors still have currency. Folk going north on the A1 could be told *'Turn left at the Scotch Corner Hotel to get to Carlisle'* or if on the A19 *'It's close to the Cleveland Tontine'*.

Pubs were navigational markers and the Boot and Shoe was one of many such along the A1. A major road junction was an obvious place for an Inn. In coaching days a chance to rest, water and maybe change your horse. In modern times rest and refreshment were equally welcome.

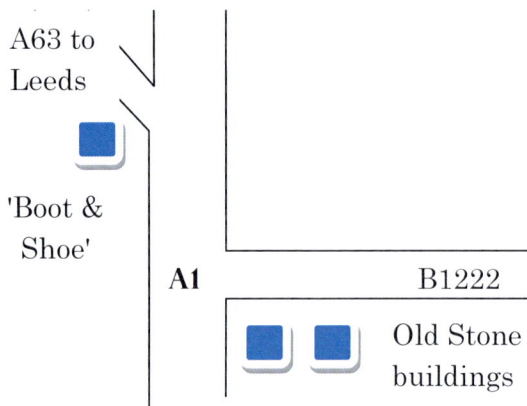

A63 to Leeds

'Boot & Shoe'

A1

B1222

Old Stone buildings

Latterly a lorry park, the 'Boot and Shoe' only ceased to be a pub in the early years of the 21st century. It was situated close to the road sign on the left of the picture on the previous page. Given that the B1222's slip road on the A1 joins just south of the former pub, that would seem "case solved". That the pub was on the far side of the A1 and a little north of the original junction seemed minor impediments - but that would be to ignore the buildings that are actually in the crook of the A1/B1222 junction

Looking at the records, and asking the local South Milford Parish Council, there was indeed an Inn at the junction, but one called the 'Pointer Inn' not the 'Boot and Shoe'. Victorian census records show it as a farm, whilst maps are insistent that it is an Inn. It seems entirely possible that it can have been both - combining a bit of smallholding and a bit of brewing in an outhouse, ready to welcome travellers and at a pinch put up a few for the night in a hay loft.

It clearly was sufficiently important a venue to act as a legal setting. Historian Edward French from the Parish Council informs me of an event from the 1860s as follows: "*The Inn is famous for a murder enquiry that occurred in Ledsham. A farm labourer was beaten to death by navvies residing in the area whilst building the railway. The inquest was held at the Inn and an offender named, from Ireland I believe. A court case followed and the offender was acquitted. I believe it was a dispute over a girl.*".

That seems to me to argue that, originally, it would have been more correct to describe the B1222 as running between Fulford, and the Pointer Inn, South Milford. The line of the road as it approaches the A1 is, in part, the parish boundary as it was at Bishopwood.

Having found that anomaly, I looked on Victorian maps to see if there was anything else to glean. To my surprise, there was further evidence to suggest that maybe the path of the B1222 didn't end here. On the far side of the A1, but more or less in direct line with the B1222, was a public footpath. The thought occurred that, perhaps in the days before motor vehicles, this really was a crossroads, not a junction. An east/west local path meeting a north/south trunk route - what better to have at a junction than a hostelry?

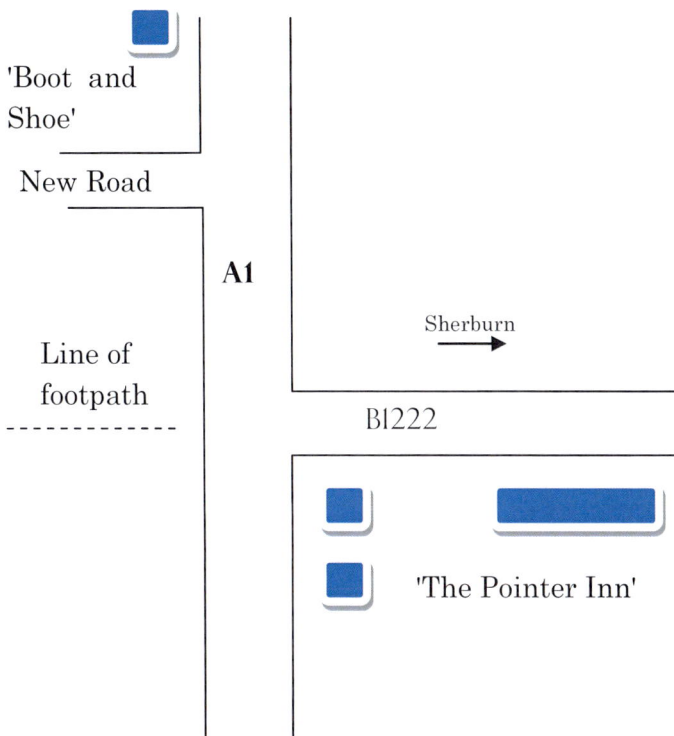

'Boot and Shoe'

New Road

A1

Line of footpath

Sherburn →

B1222

'The Pointer Inn'

This footpath leads down to the village of Ledsham, which is also the destination of 'New Road' that branches off the A1 a little further north. Hypothesising a little more, if this was a 'new road', is it possible to guess that the original line of the B1222 as shown by the surviving footpath was, for some reason, rejected in favour of a new tarmaced road that skirts around the adjacent field?

If the track that became the B1222 really did follow the footpath line once across the A1, it would have terminated at Ledsham. Stretching imagination still further, Ledsham seems a fairly small place to call a halt. Only a few miles further west lies the Roman Ridge Road, the A656.

Perhaps the B1222's footpath forebear went all the way to that highway. In which case we can dream of part of a Roman Legion 'taking the scenic route' for a Sunday stroll along a precursor of the B1222 from Lagentium (or, as we call it, Castleford) to Eboracum (that's York, of course).

The Pointer Inn seems to have stopped being a licensed premises around the time of the major reorganisation of the junction in the early1960s. As the B1222 was now kept separate from the A1, perhaps the new layout made chance visits less easy to achieve. Perhaps the loss of farmland made the operation unviable.

The buildings remain, and are now a kennels, dog training centre and automotive repair depot. As can be seen from the frontage behind the fence on the image on page 114, there is evidence of an archway that may have been large enough in earlier times to allow horses through into a stables area to the rear. The diagram below describes the way in which the A1/A63 and the B1222 now meet. All in all quite a complex - but entirely necessary - geometry to allow a link road to connect to its trunk in the 21st century.

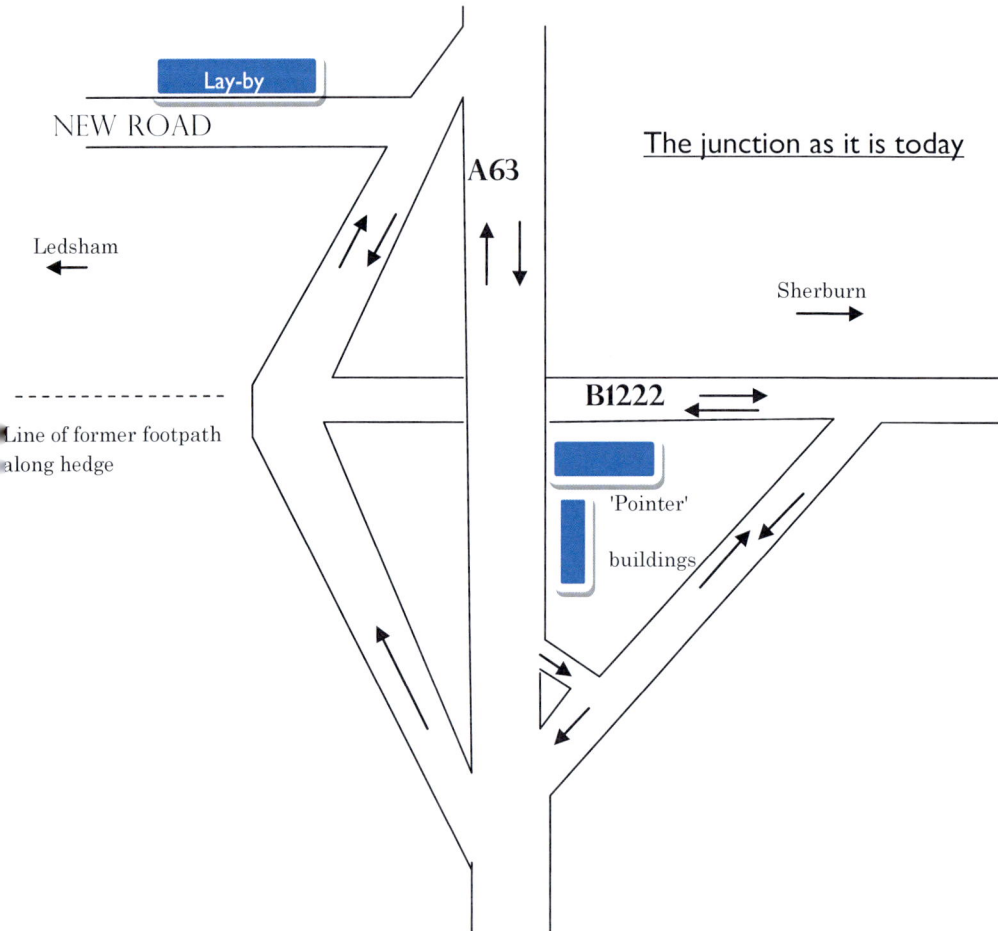

Lay-by

NEW ROAD

The junction as it is today

A63

Ledsham

Sherburn

B1222

Line of former footpath along hedge

'Pointer'

buildings

People who are regular users of this stretch of road will know there is an entire step in the evolution of the junction that I have missed out. In the 1960s, the A63 was extended to 'fly over' the A1. If you wanted to go southbound onto the B1222 you had an unnerving manoeuvre to carry out - get on to the A1 from the A63 slip, only to exit onto the B1222

100 yards later. This may well have been the isolation of the 'Pointer' that caused its downfall. Whilst the B1222 slip road still exists, in the further remodernization of the junction in the 2000s, the flyover and its scary descent onto the A1 has totally gone, with the line of the slip marked merely by a grassy verge.

*The frontage of the Pointer Inn/Farm buildings, and B1222 slip looking south, 2020*

**<u>The junction area is a hazardous environment</u>**. If you must, the **<u>only sensible place</u>** to take in the geometry is to park in a small, unofficial lay-by on the north side of New Road and look at things from there.

To go north, the B1222 dives under the old A1 and emerges via a slip road onto the northbound carriageway. **<u>This slip road is a two-way road.</u>**  New Road branches off just before that slip joins the main road.

To leave the A1 when going south, or to join from the B1222 to go further south, a new slip road was built through part of the **Poin**ter Inn's land.

 It is **<u>very important</u>** to note that the roads and junctions are **<u>very busy</u>** with **<u>high speed traffic</u>** probably not looking out for pedestrians or dawdling, history-checking motorists.

At this juncture, the journey is complete : except for one more, rather personal, reference.

# Harry Lauder's view

In the introduction I described how much of the inspiration for the book was that I have lived on or near the B1222 for most of my adult life, and thus I wanted to share the 'joys and sorrows' of living by the road. To those of a certain football bent, that 'joys and sorrows' line points up the other inspiration for the book : that of the 'theme song' of my football club, Birmingham City. The illustration on page 7 referred to the 'ends of the road'.

Harry Lauder's song 'Keep Right on to the End of the Road' is Birmingham's 'theme song' In the chorus, Lauder, whom Winston Churchill called 'Scotland's Greatest Ever Ambassador', sings:

*Keep right on to the end of the road,*
*Keep right on to the end,*
*If the way be long, let your heart be strong,*
*Keep right on round the bend.*
*If you're tired and weary still journey on,*
*Till you come to your happy abode,*
*Where all you love that you're dreaming of*
*Will be there at the end of the road.*

The journey's surely not so extended that you've become tired and weary, I hope you've managed to find your way around the bends of the B1222, and I realise a complex road junction is hardly something that many dream of at the end of a road. But in 'Keeping On..' I hope you have appreciated and enjoyed some part of my personal travelogue.

*Harry Lauder in 1909 (courtesy Wiki)*

# Reference Section : Websites, Books and Societies

Googling any particular item on the itinerary will bring up lots of sites, and wiki will add to those. So the sites I've listed here are perhaps more 'hidden'. Websites were live and addresses correct in late 2020, but as with all things on line that could change

## Websites

Athelstan's palace https://historicengland.org.uk/listing/the-list/list-entry/1017486

Battle of Fulford   www.battleoffulford.org.uk  (a little out of date, but still of interest)

Bell Hall, Naburn : https://historicengland.org.uk/listing/the-list/list-entry/1296999

Cawood Treasure Trail : www.treasuretrails.co.uk/things-to-do/north-yorkshire/cawood

Colour and letter schemes for road signs
https://assets.publishing.service.gov.uk/government/uploads/system/uploads/attachment_data/fil
e/782725/traffic-signs-manual-chapter-07.pdf      Or, google "DfT Traffic Signs Manual" (over
200 pages long!) and go to chapter 7.

Elmet genes   www.nature.com/news/uk-mapped-out-by-genetic-ancestry-1.17136

Historic Ordnance Survey maps : National Library of Scotland https://maps.nls.uk/os/

Naburn Hospital Site   www.countyasylums.co.uk/naburn-fulford-york/

Naburn images and local history     www.naburnvillage.org

Naburn Hall   https://britishlistedbuildings.co.uk/101167205-naburn-hall-
naburn#.X8UdXmX7TlU

Naburn water treatment plant   www.yorkpress.co.uk/news/4580741.taking-a-tour-around-
yorks-sewerage-treatment-works-at-naburn/

Road diagrams and information  : www.roads.org.uk

Road history
https://web.archive.org/web/20110724050836/http://www.cbrd.co.uk/indepth/roadnumbers/hist
ory.shtml

Scalm Park control tower  : https://historicengland.org.uk/listing/the-list/list-entry/1020499

Sherburn Airfield  : www.airfields-in-yorkshire.co.uk/sherburn/

Sherburn Local History : www.sherburninelmethistory.co.uk/

Squires' Cafe  : www.squires-cafe.co.uk/about/history-of-squires/

Steeton Gateway : https://archive.org/details/YAJ021/page/242/mode/2up

Steeton Gateway : www.english-heritage.org.uk/visit/places/steeton-hall-gateway/history/

Stillingfleet Parish  : www.british-history.ac.uk/vch/yorks/east/vol3/pp101-112#highlight-first

St. Helen's Stillingfleet : www.greatenglishchurches.co.uk/html/stillingfleet.html  *and*
www.britainexpress.com/counties/yorkshire/churches/stillingfleet.htm

## Books and articles

Baring Gould, S. : *Yorkshire Oddities* (Bishopwood Tale)

Bogg, E. : *The Old Kingdom of Elmet.* (pub 1902 : Long out of print, available via the internet)

Booth, J. : *The Day War Broke Out* (Tales of Cawood Bridge in WW2. Long out of print.)

Brown, T.W. : *The Making of a Yorkshire Village : Thorner* (Elmet matters)

Butler, D. : *1066 : The Story of a Year* (Battle of Fulford)

Crossley, E.W; Kitson, S. D. : 'Steeton Hall', *Yorkshire Archaeological Journal*, 21 (1911), 203–10

Hartley, K.E. : *The Cawood, Wistow and Selby Light Railway*

King, H.F. : *Sopwith Aircraft 1912-1920* (Blackburn Aircraft)

Morris. J. : *Age of Arthur*  (Elmet matters)

Wood, M. : *In Search of the Dark Ages* (Athelstan)

Guides to All Saints' Sherburn - available from the church

Yorkshire Archaeological Society : *Yorkshire Boundaries*

## Societies (all of whom have an internet presence)

Cawood Garth Group

Fulford Community Orchard

Local History Societies based at Barwick in Elmet, Fulford, Naburn and Sherburn in Elmet.

SABRE (The Society for All British Road Enthusiasts)